THIS BOOK IS A GIFT FROM

THE FRIENDS OF THE WEST LAFAYETTE PUBLIC LIBRARY

2010

A BOOK IS A TREASURE TO OPEN AGAIN AND AGAIN

# The Scroll of Anatiya

# The Scroll of Anatiya

ZOË GRASHOW KLEIN

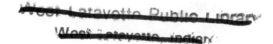
RESOURCE *Publications* · Eugene, Oregon

THE SCROLL OF ANATIYA

Resource Publishing
A Division of Wipf and Stock Publishers
199 W. 8th Ave., Suite 3
Eugene, OR 97401

www.wipfandstock.com

ISBN 13: 978-1-60608-543-1

Manufactured in the U.S.A.

4/10 Amazon 22.00

www.zoeklein.com
www.drawinginthedust.com

# Author's Note

*The Scroll of Anatiya* is a work of fiction.
Like dreams.
Which are metaphors for other stuff which may or may not be real.

# Translator's Note

As is well known from the detailed account in *Drawing in the Dust* (Simon and Schuster, 2009), the items excavated at the ancient site of Anatot, a suburb of Jerusalem, by team ANAT XIIV, led by respected archaeologist Page Brookstone of Columbia University, were extraordinary and explosive. It matched, some say, the historic and literary significance of the Dead Sea Scrolls discovered in 1947, but if one were to measure the finds based on condition of scrolls *as well as content*, the discovery of the complete Scroll of Anatiya might fairly be considered unrivaled.

In what seemed to be a small shrine carved out of the eastern wall of a deep cistern, Brookstone discovered a cache of three scrolls. The scrolls included Jeremiah, Lamentations, and a hitherto unknown scroll now referred to as Anatiya. Among the three scrolls are three distinct handwriting styles, and it is already consensus opinion to refer to these scribes as Anatiya, Baruch, and Ben Sira.

Attributed to Anatiya are chapters 1 through 51 of the Scroll of Anatiya, excluding the last paragraph of chapter 51. Attributed to Baruch are the scrolls of Jeremiah, Lamentations, and the last paragraph of chapter 51 of Anatiya. Attributed to Ben Sira is chapter 52 of Anatiya, which is written in Hebrew with a number of Greek loan-words.

Also found in the shrine were the skeletal remains of two people, one male and the other female, with their arms around each other and their ribs overlapping, as cards being shuffled. These remains have been dated to the mid-to-late sixth century BC.

The author of the Scroll of Anatiya, a passionate follower of the prophet Jeremiah, was born ca. 620 BC. She witnessed the capture and destruction of Jerusalem in 587, was released by the Babylonians from the Israelite exiles to return to Israel, witnessed the murder of Gedaliah, the appointed governor of Jerusalem, in 586, and survived the ensuing Chaldean attack. She joined the small number of Israelite exiles to Egypt and lived there from 586–585, after which she returned to Anatot, where her life ended ca. 583.

Those readers familiar with Jeremiah will note the obvious similarities between the text of his prophecies and this text. There is a striking symmetry of structure in the outline of the chapters. The two authors frequently discuss the same historic events. Often phrases and entire verses are shared by both texts, and it is unclear whether certain phrases originate with Anatiya or with Jeremiah. Similarly, our text weaves phrases from Torah (the Five Books of Moses), the two Books of Samuel, the two Books of Kings, Proverbs, Psalms, The Song of Songs, Job, and selections from the prophets. Excepting where texts obviously predate 629 (readers beware: literary chronology rarely predicts date of authorship!) it requires serious consideration to discern the author's intentional allusions, text that is original to her, and wording that may have been idiom of the time.

While another translator might have chosen to publish the text side by side with Jeremiah in order to facilitate comparisons, I prefer to let Anatiya's voice remain autonomous. I have also chosen not to burden this initial version of the text with extensive annotation and footnotes. The text itself does demand scholarly study, and there is no doubt that supplemented editions will soon follow. The point of this edition is merely to recover an extraordinary ancient voice and to render it accessible to the modern reader.

Before turning to the text I must remind readers that all efforts to make unfamiliar worlds and characters speak to a modern reader, whether in translation or in fiction, require simultaneously a commitment to fidelity and a burst of imagination. Having said this, let me acknowledge that in a number of cases, where Hebraicisms were unmatched in other known texts and simpler renderings seemed to miss the leaps the author intended to make, I chose to use a more modern translation to indicate the urgency of context. Examples include: **metaphor** (*ot-hashpa'a*), which may have more literally translated as "sign of influence"; **potentiality** and **actuality** (*sh'yecholet, sh'ma-kayam*), "what could be and what matter exists"; **ego** (*ha'ani*), "the I"; **paranoia**, simply *yira*, is the common word for fear, but I based my choice on the qualifiers *einai-chetz*, which I rendered *darting-eye*, literally "arrow-eyes"; **chant** (*hazara-hazara*), "repeat-repeat"; and **infinity** (*blisof*), "without end."

Many of the difficulties I encountered have been met by biblical translators countless times before. For example, there is an old controversy over the translation "dolphin skin," which appears in the book of Leviticus describing the material used to construct the Tabernacle. Some say a better translation would simply be "tarp"; after all, what did these desert nomads know of dolphins? Rather than risk my translation being used as a commentary in an outdated debate, I opted for "dolphin skin" here as well. As another example, the word *hashmal* is left untranslated in many renditions of Ezekiel. In modern Hebrew it means "electricity," but seemed to refer to some sort of glowing amber rock.

Another challenge occurred when Jeremiah is imprisoned, in my translation, by "a man named Fear." I debated whether to translate the jailer's name, *Iriya*, which literally means fear. I worry I may have overstepped my bounds here, rendering this segment more symbolic and less historic. Finally, I can't resist pointing out that *Milushari*, the name Anatiya gives her place of dream and fantasy, in Hebrew letters is Jerusalem written backwards.

I am well aware of the trend in translation to render ancient text in gender-neutral language, but I concluded, quite confidently, that the ingenuity and uniqueness of Anatiya's voice is only enhanced when we honestly understand the dominant male God-concept to which her culture adhered. I also chose to capitalize all nouns, pronouns, and epithets referring to God so as to maintain the integrity of belief at that time.

The original scroll moves back and forth from a poetical to a narrative style. For the most part, I followed the familiar JPS version of Jeremiah in moving between styles of presentation. The only time I broke with JPL was in chapter 13, where the lyrics describing Jeremiah's body were so poetical they seemed best rendered in verse.

The least poetical verses posed the most difficulty in translation, namely Baruch's speech, which was characterized in the original as halting in a way that reads haltingly. The author used unusual techniques when recording conversations with Baruch, including stand-alone *alefs*, which have been rendered as "um," and words that seem to stutter, such as *ani-ni*. In Anatiya we also find the last letters of Baruch's words smeared into the first letters of the words that follow, suggesting a slurred sort of speech. The translation tries to capture the characterization the author made every effort to depict. A note about the handwriting: Anatiya's handwriting is not nearly as consistent or as artful as that of Baruch or Ben Sira. Over the course of her scroll it changes from tightly wound, small letters to a looser, more languidly flowing, downward sloping script. Throughout, however, is her signature letter *yud*, which has three little sweeps at the top.

The historical value of this piece is indisputable. A passage describing King Josiah provides exciting proof text that the scroll mentioned in the Book of Kings II long suspected to be Deuteronomy, the fifth of the five books of Moses, actually *is* Deuteronomy. The small group of scholars that have long held that Deuteronomy was in fact composed by Jeremiah and Baruch here find powerful textual basis for these claims. Anatiya lends tremendous historicity to such figures as Ezekiel, lesser known prophets as Hanamel and Uriah, priestly figures such as Pashhur and Zephania. Past archeological discoveries, including the "Seal of Baruch" found in 1975, and the soldered "I love you" amulets and bracelets discovered throughout the Jezreel valley, here find resource as well. The scroll contributes to the completion of the picture we have of this region and era, with its mention of hitherto unreferenced sites such as Coffee Alley and Baker's Street, its brief tour of the palace and Temple, as well as its references to unknown texts such as the hidden books of Anatot and letters written by Anatiya to her son. It goes without saying that Anatiya makes an immeasurable contribution to filling out the historic landscape. How could we have ever read Jeremiah's letter to the exiles, portions of Ezekiel, or for that matter, the entire Books of Lamentations and Jeremiah, without this clarifying, captivating, and complicated voice? Simultaneously, of course, the Scroll of Anatiya raises as many, if not more, questions than it answers.

As valuable as Anatiya is historically, the literary value of the scroll can never be dismissed. It maps an internal landscape of emotion and desire with as much, if not more, precision than it details historic events. It cannot fairly be compared to any other known text of its time. The romantic and erotic Song of Songs is clearly a compilation of sonnets, although there are those who would argue it is the story of two lovers over a period of time. The Book of Ruth and the Book of Judith are both character- and plot-driven, but never escape the agenda of their redactors. Anatiya is a first person, honest, and vulnerable account of an orphaned, passion-driven disciple of Jeremiah, perhaps a prophetess in her own right, composed as an epic love poem in which an immensely personal philosophy is expressed and nurtured, and in which a political agenda is subtle and noncompetitive with the overarching themes. It remains the most character-driven and thematic of any known Hebraic text, more comparable to certain Greek epics of a later date. Anatiya is a rare window into an incredible world and a beautiful mind, and what emerges, out of this century of war, wrath, starvation, and exile is a timeless theology of love that is sure to redefine trends in the history of mankind and thought.

I present to you the first complete English translation of the Scroll of Anatiya.

Jordanna Lamm
The Missing Page, Inc.
An Intuitive Translation Service

# 1

THE WORDS OF ANATIYA, daughter of Avigayil, one of the handmaids at the temple at Anatot in the territory of Benjamin. ²She fell deeply in love with Jeremiah in her thirteenth year. ³Her body was so faint with love for Jeremiah that her soul caught in her throat and made her mute for the remainder of her days. ⁴In the quietude of her love, she penned the songs of her heart. ⁵She shadowed Jeremiah all of his days like a faint aroma of meadow, like a distant memory of lilies abloom in the valley of Sharon. ⁶A child-spook, a brittle tea-leaf, she hid within her a passion for the prophet Jeremiah that was silver-trumpet-loud.

⁷The moment I saw you I knew:

That I had been destined for you when my soul was yet on high;
before I was a swell in my mother's belly, I was consecrated
to be the one to love you as a desert flower loves a drop of dew.

⁸I saw you
surrounded with God
and I fell upon my face
and praised God, and blessed you,
⁹and I knew that surely I would die
should I lift my eyes and see
the Holy One face to face,
¹⁰but I heard your brave little voice
as a clear glass bell ring out:
"Ah, Lord God,
I don't know how to speak!"

¹¹I lifted my eyes,
I could not help myself!

Your voice stirred me so.
[12]I looked up and saw you
standing at God's very core,
and you were not consumed!
[13]No, you radiated like a beacon
in a pure star-dewy mist,
your skin was translucent,
luminous,
a veil of sunlight over
a sky-blue soul.
[14]Your eyes were two black moons
sailing through your open face,
Your skin gleamed like a polished marble floor.
[15]Your ears were small
as a newborn's open palms,
snatching at God's words,
which filled the air like thin bubbles.

[16]You dazzled me.
I opened my mouth to cry out to you,
and the God that surrounded you streamed into my throat, swelling
      my soul.
[17]I thought I might die, but I lost my voice instead of my life

~WROTE ANATIYA.


[18]When God put out a hand and touched your mouth,
God put out another hand,
and touched the tip of a finger to my lips,
whispering, "Shhhh." [19]I never spoke again.
But I would gladly give my tongue, Jeremiah,
if I might be your life companion,
that I might be your quiet rose
among the damsels of the land.

[20]I tucked almond blossoms into my hair
and scratched your name with a twig under my thigh,
over and over until it scarred,
that my body might never forget whilst she slept
the one whom my soul loves.

[21]I set my pot on the fire
and the steam curled away
from the heat in my fingers.
[22]My fingers could have been fire-sticks.
They dripped thick myrrh as candles running wax,
longing, forgive me, to touch.
[23]I was quick to stir tea
and warm up the rocks that I might bake cakes for you.
[24]I took three measures of flour and hastily kneaded.
[25]My fingers spread outward over the dough,
wings of a white dove a-flutter.
[26]I baked you honey cakes with crumbled mint
and I left them by your door every morning,
and so my fingers touch you

~WROTE ANATIYA.

[27]At night I lay awake on my couch.
This love threw me sandward into a swoon
countless times throughout the day
and I began to feel myself pale and unearthly.
[28]I wondered whether I was human at all,
or whether—God forgive me one untamed thought!—
perhaps I myself was an angel,
muted so as not to distract from my singular mission:
[29]to sustain my love with cakes
and protect the embers of his precious light.
[30]Or perhaps I am just sick with love
and this fever keeps my feet just over this land
so that I hover like a gold-laced cloud,
dizzy and tearful,

clinging for my dear life
to a mountaintop.

[31]I might kiss you never,
but if I could save you but once,
if I could be there one time
to throw my body before a poisoned dart,
[32]if I could be there one time only
to eat up your depression
and die of it in your place,
it would be sweeter to my soul than a kiss.
No treasure could match it

~WROTE ANATIYA.

## 2

Even as a youth,
before the flower of my maidenhood had bloomed,
I have been devoted to you; your secret bride
whom you did not know.

[2]When my desire pierced me
like a wreath of thorns around my head,
and when the pain was sharp behind my eyes,
I escaped into the wilderness
and filled my arms with nature's harvest.
[3]I stretched out in beds of blossoms
until my skin was pressed with petals.
[4]I tromped barefooted, plowing the soil with my toes.
[5]At the height of my sickness for you, Jeremiah,
I threw my arms around a sturdy tree
and my legs over a stubby branch,
and, [6]O God! Let my piety remain intact!
[7]I assure you no man has known me, my dear,
but that tree did break my virgin seal.
I kissed its wooden heart

~WROTE ANATIYA.

[8]My father did leave when I was a child.
He had chewed on my mother's heart,
sucked it like a cluster of purple grapes through his teeth,
but she still eked out some love for me.

[9]Never did I ask her "Where is my father?"
[10]What need had I of frightful eyes and a beard of thorns?
[11]Purple cloth has the high price of gold
yet my mother was clothed in purple for free,
like swollen leeches under her skin.
She was my mother-queen.

[12]He abandoned us
and at five I did the work of a bondsman,
bearing bundles on my shoulders like a pack mule,
teetering and scraping along the corners of the farmers' fields.
[13]My sapling-thighs strained like an ox,
rolling a stone wheel to grind that wheat into flour.
[14]My mother made loaves to sell to merchants.

[15]She wept over my neck
which was too young and might break
under the weighty water jugs
I bore home atop my head.
[16]My neck was lovely and slender as a bride's wrist
peeking out from under ceremonial wraps.

[17]I grew cedar-strong and sun-callused,
black as the tents of Kedar,
industrious as an insect dragging twice its weight
with its wispy baby-hair legs.
[18]On my mat I dreamt toil
so that my sleep was sore and physical,
little less than the days.
[19]I heard the buzz of heat and the silence loud

and the sun struck me dizzy
so that, I am ashamed O Lord!
[20]I sometimes stole a suck from a she-goat's teat
when her shepherd looked away.
[21]The iniquity of a child, dear Lord,
if I am guilty, I stand accused

~WROTE ANATIYA.


[22]I did find my mother
the day she died.
[23]I found my fount of living waters
seeping redly into Sheol.
[24]I chipped the dough-flakes from her hands
and tucked poppies under her low breasts,
two broken cisterns
that cannot even hold water.
[25]I wept.
I dragged her on her mat with my two hands,
walking backwards, my bird-back hunched,
my cries raised up.
[26]I scuffled her to the grave I dug,
like a little ant dragging a fragment of honeycomb
six times its weight, clenched in pinching jaw,
jerking it under the ground.
[27]My head was bare.


I sat between heaven and death,
an avalanche of hurt ran down my chest,
tears, and the tremble of heartbreak.
[28]Good-bye my queen,
my earthly sovereign.
Heaven help me little me,
I was utterly dazed

~WROTE ANATIYA.

<sup>29</sup>I must have done a twofold wrong
to have driven away my father
and lost my mother's spirit.
<sup>30</sup>Forgive me, O Heaven,
my presence is no salve,
my touch no healing balm.
<sup>31</sup>But know, Lord, as much
as this damaged vessel can bear,
with its fissures and leaks,
that awe for You is in me!
Awe for You is in me!

~WROTE ANATIYA.


<sup>32</sup>God speaks to you, Jeremiah,
with hot-iron words God strikes you.
<sup>33</sup>God brands you with the Most High disappointment.
God tears a fissure in the firmament
and lets loose the skies' ocean upon your soul.
<sup>34</sup>Ocean-tossed boy,
I am your Constant.
<sup>35</sup>Here, ducked down and timorous,
here-ever, here-after
a moon-pebble caught in your small orbit
twining forever here,
after there are no words left
falling in tumult from the Throne
and God turns away to tend
an underground spring in the desert,
here am I still constant
while age picks at me with tiny fingers.
I fear not. <sup>36</sup>Love is strong as death.


<sup>37</sup>My desire rolls over me and flattens my bones.
<sup>38</sup>A frosty hand grabs hold of my heart

and you appear to me as a warm shaft of light.
I am sick! I am sick for you, prophet!
[39]I run to a high hill while tears slant from my eyes,
I might leap, I just might!
[40]I scramble upward to the hilltop.
This lust is too base, too alien,
it wants to bury me young!
[41]I must climb straight above it.
At the top my throat is closing.
[42]My fingertips are swollen and pulsing.
[43]O Lord, how you have fashioned restlessness in this young girl!
[44]It is no use.
I wrap my legs around a verdant tree
like well-watered vines.
Its branches enfold my back lightly.
A young leafy shoot reaches out.
[45]My arms woven amidst its branches,
my hands grasping tight,
I lifted myself up,
(O forgive me Blessed Watcher!)
[46]my mouth did open
and I pressed my dry tongue to the bark
and I loved and I said
to the tree, [47]"you are my lover."
And I cried for salvation
and the tree, it shook with the weight of me.

[48]I curled up, dear Lord, and I cried until dawn.
My love has driven me mad.
I call You to save me, to account for my soul.
[49]Do not stone me for my thirst!
Do not drop Your fists of hail upon me!
[50]Do not turn Your back on me, O Lord!
[51]I vow that no man will know me,
no man will know me, but the trees,

do forgive this palest of iniquities,
the desert trees will bear marks of my teeth

~WROTE ANATIYA.

[52]You are sitting on a flat stone in the valley
listening to the shining words of the Lord.
[53]They come to you strung together in furious poetry.
I stand by and gather handfuls of spilt syllables
which roll away like forgotten jewels,
round and smooth over the white face of sand.
[54]I wear them around my neck.

[55]Your hair is raven black, slick as feathers,
and the afternoon sunlight is reflected in your locks
as a glowing ring of amber light
that cascades gently over your shoulders.
[56]Your skin is a sheen over a shadow,
a bright over a dark.
[57]Should the dark side of the moon
surface with the bright, this would be your pallor.
[58]Your eyes are the first day of Creation.
In them, God separated the light from the darkness.
[59]God called the light "Eye,"
and the darkness God called "Iris."
[60]Your lips are the deepening horizon.
[61]The blue veins on your wrists
are a perfect map of the rivers of Eden.
Here is Pishon and her sister Gihon,
winding up the length of your arm, side by side.
[62]And here branches Tigris and here branches Euphrates,
and here your lifeblood courses
from your upturned hand, a tiny Eden,
from hand to head, from head to hand,
and heart, and love,
[63]if I could kiss you now

just one place, it would be there,
upon your delicate palm.
[64]And then upon your neck and inside your setting-sun mouth,
for no, I could never kiss you just one place my love.
I could kiss you never,
but never just once

~WROTE ANATIYA.

3

If I were your wife I would hide my blush behind a veil of sky. I'd need
no embroidered garment, no band of gold. [2]And if you should look at
my fingers and ask, "My love, with what shall I adorn these hands, these
almond blossoms?" [3](for so I imagine your speaking), then I would say,
[4]"Carve for me your third eye, the one that shows you visions of the Lord,
genuine from under your brow, and I shall wear it upon my finger. It is the
gem with the most excellent clarity."

[5]But fantasy is for the unworthy.
You must know that I am a desert nymph,
whoring with the foliage.
[6]The trees straighten up
in reverence to me.
[7]How I myself despise.
It is because of me that they become
brittle and chapped, those blameless sprouts.
[8]When no cloud offers respite,
and no rain quenches their wooden hearts,
it is because I have laid a curse upon them,
tainted their sap with my own.
[9]Hard-working ants march up to the spot
to investigate the sweet mingling
of girl-child and resin.
[10]Dear Father, water your garden!
Do not mind me as I lie among the sticks.

[11]Jeremiah is the companion of my youth,
and I am only his shadow's shadow.
[12]Do not withhold the Heaven's late showers
on account of such a forgotten dream,
such a forgettable dreamer as me.

[13]Josiah was eight years old when he became king, nearly twenty years before my birth. [14]I imagine him then, as little and lean as I today, nestling himself into that wide golden throne. [15]Sweet Josiah, noble and pure, love of your mother, Jedidah daughter of Adaiah descendent of David. She was named for the psalmist's own son. [16]Your father sacrificed unclean animals to chipped idols, pounded his breast in painted temples. [17]You were old enough to remember when your father's own courtiers murdered him and the people of the land did then massacre them. [18]With the bloodied hands and thirsty eyes of wolves, they lifted you upon the chair. [19]A people awaited your rulership, while you sadly consented to overcome your years. [20]A shepherd from a little lamb was forged. O, your eight years must have seemed to you as eight branches of Temple light, filled with oil and set on fire! ~wrote Anatiya.

[21]You found a companion in Shaphan the scribe. He delivered you a message from on high. [22]He proclaimed: "I have found a scroll of the Teaching in the House of the Lord!" [23]And Shaphan read to you as Jedidah did when your childhood was still a gift. [24]He read, "These are the words that Moses addressed to all Israel on the other side of the Jordan." [25]You did not stir, you barely blinked all the while he read, all through the night by a dim oil lamp. Your heart leapt when he read "O happy Israel!" and a moment later you wept when he read, "He buried him." [26]As he ended the scroll, in that tiny moment, the Lord showed the whole land to you. [27]It was cringing and crying to you. You tore your garment, wept and stood. [28]You trusted no man at that time, and so you sought the wisdom of a woman, the prophetess Hulda. [29]Her husband was the keeper of the wardrobe, and he was knowledgeable in robing. But she was knowledgeable in disrobing. [30]She knew to peel away the thick husks and see to the clear kernel of truth within. She showed you the word of the Lord ~wrote Anatiya.

[31]The Lord set you ablaze with anger toward those other altars. [32]There was a fraction of Moses within you when you flared up against each and every wild golden calf. [33]You hated the parade which tore with

glitter-teeth at your carefully sown gardens, galloping through your royal orchards where the voice of God was known to stroll. [34]There was a fraction of Noah within you when you invited the waters to purge the land. [35]You ground the bones of the priests and burned them on their altars. [36]You hewed down the incense stands and the shrines of the gates, turned Ashera and Ashtoreth into dust, demolished the Baals and the cubicles of male prostitutes. [37]You burned the chariots of the sun and froze the fires of Molech, so that no child should be tossed into that raging pit. [38]You melted molten images into precious rivulets until the land bled silver, copper, and fine gold.

[39]O beautiful Josiah, you turned to the Lord with all of your heart and soul and might. [40]The Lord swore that no disaster should befall whilst your good eyes still shine. But it has been said that you will be slain before your time, plucked early from your place so that you should not see God's wrath. [41]But I shall see it, and I shall live it. O protect our righteous King Josiah that the day may not come! [42]Hulda did not tell you all that she saw, Josiah. [43]She knew your end and hid the words, "Beware the river Euphrates!" ~wrote Anatiya.

[44]The icy moon removed her hood,
thinking that she was alone. So small are we
to her that she mistakes us for empty space.

[45]You turn back the cover while you sleep
and I see your shoulder, round and bare,
luminous as the water's moon-reflections.
[46]So unlike any man, Jeremiah,
you are dust of stars, ashes of the silvery moon.

[47]I have resolved to adopt you as my life,
and I offer you my presence
which shies away in love.
[48]I offer you my faint, vaporous presence,
that you might ever-suspect
you are fiercely loved.
[49]I tumble to you, an uprooted weed,

over undulating hills.
⁵⁰Let us lie down in our weariness
and let my breath be a cover to you,
warm and sweet as a field
where you dream of sweeping trees
and silence.


# 4


Return your soul, O prophet

~WROTE ANATIYA.


²Return your soul
from its celestial academy
where angels read praises
by the light she emits.
³Return your soul,
restless sleeper,
from its wandering on high.
⁴At night our bodies peek into the kingdom of death.
⁵Return your soul, O prophet,
let day not break without your return,
that nations might bless themselves by you,
that holiness might not flee our realm.

⁶I adjure you men of Judah and Jerusalem, do not scorn me!
I am powerless at the end of desire's short leash.

⁷Boars snuff for truffles in the dust.
Children scuffle for coins in the sand.
⁸Treasure hunters and grave robbers
tunnel a labyrinth through Sheol.
⁹All eyes comb the footpath for
a gem, a creeping herb, an antler for luck.
¹⁰Last night as I lay upon my mat,

my soul sought to find the one I love.
$^{11}$I walked through a damp garden
and a glisten caught my eye.
$^{12}$A drop of star, a tiger's tooth,
I crouched down to pick it up.
$^{13}$In my hand it was tiny and soft
like a baby's earlobe, and I
loved it like a baby.
$^{14}$It was the foreskin of an eight-day-old prophet.
I'd trade a truffle, a coin, a treasure
to any finder's keeper for the piece of you
their flint-stone sheared away.
$^{15}$This is the key to your covenant with Heaven,
I held it aloft to the moon.
$^{16}$Last night as I lay upon my mat
I found the ghost of your missing piece
and I put it into my mouth.
I chewed it delicately and
swallowed it down.
$^{17}$I woke with the taste of apples.
Jeremiah, I dream you
and I wake in a spin.

$^{18}$Citizens of Judah and Jerusalem,
cup your one heart like two hands
under a clear fountain.
$^{19}$Lift your heart to your lips
and tip your palms, drink deep.
Reshape yourselves a vessel.
$^{20}$Jeremiah's soul is an aviary
that houses every broken wing in Israel.
$^{21}$Jeremiah's heart is an atrium
in which flutters a nightmare
of chirping and squawking,
God's mad accounting.

<sup>22</sup>Perched upon an olive shoot,
one mournful bird surveys it all.
<sup>23</sup>She whistles his soul sharp
as a hot blade of grass.
<sup>24</sup>His eyes are two nets
sweeping the world's floor
and storing its lost inhabitants
in vaulted memory banks.
<sup>25</sup>My love stations a sign
with steepled letters, scrawled urgent
and with the slant of hard rain.
<sup>26</sup>The sweat of his thin brow
reflects a fevered blue flame
as he drives the post, with finality,
into the roadside as into Sisera's temple:
To Zion take refuge! Do not delay!
<sup>27</sup>Not a one can read, but I.
I studied the hidden books of Anatot

~WROTE ANATIYA.


<sup>28</sup>The tongue of the prophet strums sentences
the way the hand of the harpist strums chords.
<sup>29</sup>A heat rises to your cheeks.
In one fist you capture the ferocity of Nimrod,
in the other, the defiance of Abraham when you rail:

>  <sup>30</sup>"Ah mighty Heavens, how You deceive this people,
>  embracing them in Your right
>  with sword blazing in Your left!"

<sup>31</sup>The highest Heavens are shocked
by the thunder of this pale prophet,
which comes in full blast.
Crashing seven firmaments,

your charge unfurls like a flame against them.

[32]Tufts of cloud bandage the wound,
still I see Heaven wink an almost human tear.
[33]God loves you, Jeremiah, and your complaint
is hurtful to Him as David's sling-rock to Goliath.
[34]O save me! My breath does not come!
The sky splits and the destroyer charges out of a whirlwind
upon a horse of volcanic ash, I saw it too!
[35]Jeremiah, are we the only ones?
He is rushing toward our city on a meteor.
[36]I am stunned. I feel as if my hands have fallen to my feet.
[37]So terrifying the stain that passed over the sky,
the dark storm that filled my eyes for a blink!
[38]Steer this ship, Jeremiah, away and away
to some untouched shore, some place where the only noise
is the exploding color upon slopes of wildflowers.
[39]We are on the lip of a hungry abyss!
[40]There is a bitter freeze around my throat,
a death around my heart.
[41]Jeremiah, I saw it too, for an instant
I saw calamity utterly consume
this giant love

~WROTE ANATIYA.

[42]There is no blemish on the glow
that surrounds you like a metal shield.
[43]But what good is a shield if the hurt is inside?
It only prevents the pain from escaping.
[44]My love cries, "O my suffering, my suffering!"
[45]He falls to the ground and closes his ears between his knees
to silence the blare of horns.
[46]But the head of my love is an echo chamber
and his knees only prevent the siren from escaping.
[47]The walls of his heart strain with hurt.

O Lord, let his heart break and begin to heal
rather than this perpetual and terrible swell!
48He writhes and moans and cannot be silent.
49Dear Jeremiah, I, who am Silence, do love you.
50Were I to speak I would be swallowed by the din,
but with hushed lips I am your elixir of life.

51Your fatigue over your people wearies me.
52I pray you forgive me a wave of mild animosity
and rather admire me my honest confession:
Jeremiah, the people are not worthy of your suffering!
53They will never give you heed. They house no fear of Heaven.
54The people are love-struck through the cunning of predator gods
while here in your wake is a one,
a one who heeds your every tear,
a one who hears the soft whistle in your deep-throated sigh,
a one who envies the people your sorrow.
55Do not pity the people. They are foolish children!
Rather, pity the knowing.
A no one,
me.

56I hear an anguished cry
that severs the cord between us.
57I turn and scamper under a thicket
and clamber over a crumbling ledge.
58In the midst of this deserted ruin
lies a woman with her knees wide,
her belly ripe and a storm in her face.
59Her sleeves are drenched,
she stretches out her hand
and I crouch before her.
60My arms tremble and my head
is heavy with her musk.
She clenches a fistful of my hair

and shrieks into my neck.
[61]With hot, stinging eyes,
my fingers hook gently
like talons
under two bloody shoulders,
[62]so little, was I? was I ever this . . .
soft and afraid, arms slippery
and long as eels, dearest eyes
sealed and messy mouth
blue as early morning
without breath.
[63]"Alas for me! I faint . . ."
the woman gasps, life dimming.
I wrap my arms around her and sob
terribly. [64]With a dying hand she
urges my head toward her breast
and I suck at her sweet milk.
"Don't let it spill, not one drop,"
she says, soft, [65]my mother
is alive in my mind, in my mouth.
I weep and I drink forever, it seems.
It comes so slowly.
[66]The woman turns cold,
her faint smile and stiff
heavy fingers on the back of my neck.
My mouth is empty.

## 5

You roam the streets of this city
and I follow, close
enough for the fringe of your robe
to lap at my ankles, but far
enough for a herd of wild elephants to pass.
[2]Your eyes are searching for one

innocent memory,
when God was quiet,
nights were dreamless,
and men paid no mind.
³Your eyes are searching the city squares
while I am searching
your eyes.

⁴A branch switches at my legs
and I fall.
⁵My cheek is torn against the coarse sand
and a man's foot is hard on the small of my back.
⁶He kicks me over and I scream out:
"Jeremiah!" but no voice escapes.
He has a face harder than rock.
⁷O prophet, you roam the squares
searching for integrity,
and all the while it is trailing behind you,
⁸here inside me is integrity and goodness,
wonder and love, yet you never turn back,
you never turn and see.

⁹Is my prophet foolish?
He hears the obvious blare of horns
but is deaf to my silent cry.
¹⁰Are you not a prophet?
Can you not hear my unspoken word?

  "Jeremiah!

  "Jeremiah!

  "Jeremiah!"

[11]He takes me with bruising grip
to the ravaging tent,
beats me upon my already bleeding scalp.
[12]The branch comes down as a switch
and with each blow
I see a shock of white light.
[13]An anger wells up in my throat,
strangely, not toward him.
No, toward him I feel profound sorrow.
[14]I feel the need to explain
that he has made a mistake,
that I am everything good left in Fair Zion,
everything beautiful hidden underneath,
and he does not realize, [15]he thinks
I am just another street rat,
he does not know that I am the keeper of a love,
a love of a prophet.
[16]This is a mistake.
I can forgive a mistake.
But you ...

[17]Why should I forgive you?
You have forsaken me, Jeremiah.
[18]How is it that you listen to God
the Most Secret
and cannot intuit my longing?
[19]How is it that your eyes are filled
with the rot of this city,
and are blind to the blooming
in my heart?
[20]And how could you keep
walking and keep searching,
and how dare you
take your infatuated God with you
when I am the one,

²¹I am the one who needs Him,
and needs you, stupid prophet!
and needs help
and please rescue
my integrity
which is the
only integrity
left, in this

²²biting on my lip
and marking my neck,
²³in the corner of my eye I see a child enter the tent
and glance over at me and my destroyer,
and he sees the child too,
shoos the child away
and tears my dress.
²⁴Curse you, Jeremiah!
You have betrayed me!

~WROTE ANATIYA.


²⁵Blessed child peeks into the tent again.
The man stabs under my skirts with the branch,
²⁶a tree branch!
Of all things!
There is an insane laughter in my gut.
²⁷Good-bye God! Go on and trail Your chosen like a pup,
leaving us alone to fend off Heaven's cruelest ironies.
²⁸A light, willowy sneeze from the tent flap,
young voyeur,
awash in afternoon light
chewing on a scythe of carob.
A glance to the side,
²⁹is the child his son?
I turn and grasp a rock

and pound it once against his ear.
³⁰His son pulls back and I roll out from under.
The man twists over with a thunder in his brain
and I run.
³¹I see my legs running and remember
the long arms of the stillbirth.
Strange connections.
³²I know the man is not following me
but I am no longer running from him.
I am running from you,
³³you who have proven to be mere wind.
You who care not
if a leopard lies in wait.
³³Good-bye Jeremiah!
Cling to your God.
I shall surely forget you from afar

~WROTE ANATIYA.

³⁴I have an enduring spirit,
perhaps even an ancient spirit.
³⁵I run until my body is hollow.
A sheath of rock is before me
and vines with bitter berries creep up.
³⁶I nestle in the back of a yawning cave
and blackout sleep overtakes me.
A nightmare surfaces out of the black,
a vision out of the tar . . .
³⁷I am a fortified city.
My citizens peaceful but watchful inside.
³⁸One night, the trees pull up their roots
and gather from the surrounding hills as an army.
They batter me down with clubs.

<sup>39</sup>I scratch forty days ~ wrote Anatiya ~ into the wall of the cave. There will be no end to this solitude. <sup>40</sup>I eat berries and mushrooms and drink grassy tea. I think of Hannah's lips, moving while no voice is heard. <sup>41</sup>Eli assumed she was drunk and exiled her from the holy place. <sup>42</sup>But I know that Hannah could herself hear her voice. I talk to myself here in this cave, and my voice resonates off the walls and rings in my ears.

<sup>43</sup>The stories I tell in this cave are a violin song.
There is a wind chime in this cave; it is my laugh.
<sup>44</sup>My song is a chorus of birds.
My faintest sigh is the coo of a dove.
<sup>45</sup>But to Eli, I am mute.
To Jeremiah, I was never born.
They have ears but cannot hear!

~WROTE ANATIYA.

<sup>46</sup>And You?
You Who set the sand as a boundary to the sea?
<sup>47</sup>You by Whose wisdom the hawk
spreads his wings to the south?
<sup>48</sup>You Who know the hosts of Heaven
and call every star by name?
Do you hear me?
<sup>49</sup>Forgive me, Lord Most High!
Forgive my headstrong challenge!
<sup>50</sup>I know, now, the truth about Cain and Abel.
Don't You see?
<sup>51</sup>I love Jeremiah the way Cain loved You!
<sup>52</sup>Cain loved You and Abel kept seducing You
with gifts and plenty, and I
do love Jeremiah, and You keep seducing him
with exquisite words and daring missions,
<sup>53</sup>while all I have is this unruly vineyard
teeming with weeds and little foxes.
<sup>54</sup>O God! Do you have to be so beautiful?

[55]You Who bring the early and late rain in season,
[56]You Who paint bows of color across the mist
and beget the dewdrops,
[57]forgive my ugliness, my anger.
I am so tiresome and troublesome.
[58]Do not judge me, for I am an orphan.
[59]God knows that my deeds have been good,
but do not punish me on account of my wicked thoughts

~WROTE ANATIYA.


[60]It is an appalling and horrible thing
to be an ancient scroll,
filled with stories and secrets,
prophesies and truths,
[61]a tapestry of words sewn together
with golden thread,
hidden in an earthen jar sealed tightly,
and buried deep in a cave, in a sheath of rock,
where no one can find you, or touch you, or know you.

# 6

From the lip of my dwelling-place
I can see Jerusalem, white as snow,
gold light gleaming as a crown
on its rooftops,
curling and spilling into the streets,
[2]and at night, the moon
casts a spidery web over the city,
silver and deep blue,
in which lovers and falling stars
become entangled.

³Around the walls I can see men pitching tents.
They have weapons in their stocks
and they bide their time.
⁴As the day declines
and the shadows of evening grow long,
they gather around fires and make plans.
⁵Jerusalem knows what is coming,
and she waits there royally
and mightily.
⁶Nowhere are the shadows of evening more alluring.
Her stones are strangely tranquil.
⁷Long ago, when the followers of Korach offered offerings to the Lord
upon fire pans, the Lord's fire consumed them whole.
⁸And yet, even in the midst of the charred corpses and wailing,
the fire pans became holy.
⁹This is the secret the stones of Jerusalem know:
When the fortress is destroyed
and wickedness purged,
after the burning and the bloodlust,
even in the midst of the charred remains, ¹⁰the stones
will be holy
and eternal.

¹¹Thus says Anatiya:
Here I am hidden
in the cleft of the rock.
¹²O God, let Your goodness pass before me!
Let Your hand shield me from Your radiance,
let me gaze safely from behind
tendrils of vines!

¹³I have run like a gazelle
swiftly away from my love.
¹⁴I was afraid of being consumed like firewood
in this furnace of desire.
¹⁵It heats my chest and dries my throat.

It leaps and licks at my belly
in tiny tightened fists.
I cannot hold it in.

[16]I was afraid it would pour out,
hot as the mouth of the Leviathan,
that eruptive, boiling cauldron.
[17]Better I surrender to the cool and dank
than show my need, this monstrous thing.
[18]My sneezes flash lightning,
firebrands stream from my mouth,
and my breath ignites coals,
eyes glimmering red as dawn

~WROTE ANATIYA.


[19]I have acted shamefully
with nothing but greed in my heart.
[20]I wanted to eclipse You, God,
with my little pursed lips,
and a shrug of narrow shoulder.
[21]But is there not room enough in man
for the love of Heaven and the
affections of a mortal woman?
Or is the heart to small to bear it?
[22]O God! All is not well
with the way You have made us!
[23]Put me back, Majestic Creator,
Put me back into his breast!
I want my place by his heart.
[24]O, let Jeremiah be the first complete man
since Adam, with all of his ribs in place,
and let me be the one to complete him.
[25]I am almost bone as it is, dear Lord.
Open the spot while he sleeps
and bury me inside

~WROTE ANATIYA.

<sup>26</sup>I have run like a gazelle
swiftly away from my love
because I was afraid of the coldness
that seized my ankles
when I fell and he did not turn.
<sup>27</sup>I felt as if I were a strand of hair on his head
that had become detached.
<sup>28</sup>A hair that had come loose and slipped
from among his beautiful locks
rolling down his back,
Good-bye Jeremiah!
<sup>29</sup>I felt as insignificant,
as meaningless as a single hair
shed from a rich, black mane,
as unimportant.
<sup>30</sup>I am sick for you still.
I chew on my fingers in my anxiety.
Dear God! <sup>31</sup>My stubbornness refuses to let me go,
though I pine for the shelter of his shadow.
<sup>32</sup>I will wait many moons
and waste away
on berries and mushrooms and grassy teas
and stare flat-eyed at the Eastern gate.
<sup>33</sup>And if You should make for me this sign,
I will know there is a secret meaning
to my unclaimed life, and I shall be happy
to return to my shepherd and my love.
<sup>34</sup>And the sign shall be this:
He shall walk through that gate
and the pink morning light will cast over him a blush.
<sup>35</sup>He will take a razor to his head and shear away his locks
and cast them away, and they shall sweep upward to me,
every strand of hair. <sup>36</sup>Then I will know that he knows.
I will know I have been destined
to cherish him, here-ever, here-after,
as witness and hidden disciple,
whisper and caress.

7

Gasp! My soul leaps into my throat, I see a vision! A man in white linen is coming through the gate. [2]His head is high and lovely, O, let me gaze upon his face! [3]My eyes are saltwater fountains, pent-up springs that have just now burst. [4]He walks with a grace, with the grace of a tree, his body a white-barked tree and his hair a tumble of willowy leaves. [5]It has been nearly three moons since I have looked upon you, my life. O, your presence astonishes!

[6]Praised be God in Heaven! Praised be God on earth! Praised be God in you, dear prophet. [7]He dangles you like a lantern filled with His Own light, a light which is sown for the righteous. [8]He holds you in front of Him the way a woman holds a candle as she creeps from room to room to blow a kiss to each of her children as they lay asleep in the dark. I have been asleep! [9]For three moons I have been asleep, relying on illusions that are of no avail. [10]True, I have cleansed my body with grassy tea. I have wrestled the demons of the cliff. I have slept with a rock for my pillow. I have shaded my skin from the swarthing sun, healed my passion-wracked frame. [11]But the instant I see you appear, out of clouds of dust, I feel the sickness overtake me again, grab hold of my heart and steal my breath. I am sick for you! Sick in love! [12]I never again want to be numbly healthful. Rather, let me be filled with hurt and longing. Let me burn. [13]I feel God when I see you! I feel God racing through my veins and rousing every bit of me. [14]A shofar blasts through my body. Wake all you sleepers! Wake! I am alive, and trembling. [15]The tiny hairs on my body stand up like a troop. Praised be God for this frenzy of living!

[16]As for me, if I could just watch you ~wrote Anatiya.

[17]My spirit rushes to go to its place while my body stands dumb-founded upon the ledge. [18]When I am beside you, Jeremiah, I am an astronomer and you are the sky. Here in this cave I am the queen of the mountain, grand and glorious. [19]In your shadow I am only a speck of cinnamon dust, but the life in me is great, like the wide-leafed plant concealed within the tiny mustard seed. [20]How I rebelled against you! When I called to you and you did not respond, I doubted you. [21]Now I see you, sun-kissed, and I know . . . that here in this cave I am grand but nameless, but there in your wake I am Anatiya!

²²As for you, I hear you raise a cry of prayer on behalf of a crescent of listeners before you. Their eyes are placid and their mouths curl up half mocking. ²³In their hearts they are thinking, "Good thing he is not my son!" and "How entertaining!" ²⁴But to me, your words are delicate ice crystals fanning over the sky. ²⁵While children wander away to gather sticks, and fathers absentmindedly slow-roast leg of lamb, and mothers distract themselves with flour and water and frivolous fingers, I stand transfixed and absorbed.

²⁶How they vex you! ~wrote Anatiya. ²⁷It is rather themselves whom they vex, to their own disgrace. ²⁸But I see straight through those husks and shells and into the kernel of you. It has the gleam of amber, a fire encased in a frame. ²⁹Out of the core, torches and flares dash forth on wings. The sound of the wings is like the sound of mighty waters, and these are your words, the words of Shaddai. ³⁰They burn, and vast floods cannot quench them, nor rivers drown them.

³¹Thus writes Anatiya ~ I see that the wrath of God fills you, but the wrath is not your own. You yourself are love, Jeremiah. ³²I can see you, Jeremiah, standing boldly between God and those cities Sodom and Gomorrah, standing in Abraham's place. ³³Abraham had argued that God spare these cities if there be found a number of righteous people inside. ³⁴But you would argue differently, I know. ³⁵You would say, "Far be it from You to do such a thing, to bring death upon the people when they still might repent! ³⁶Would You wipe out the whole city if there be found one chance that a sinner might change? ³⁷What if there should be found one rebel who might turn to You in future days, turn to You and repent, will You destroy the whole city and not forgive it for the sake of one reluctant repentant? ³⁸Will the One Who created the world out of nothing, Who moved potentiality to actuality, will He ignore all potential in these large cities of living beings?"

³⁹All at once, your eyes lift, burning coals full of fever. Your eyes lift and look into my own! ⁴⁰All my life I have been the noticer, but never, until this moment, the one to be noticed. Your mouth is stilled, lips parted. ⁴¹All the world melts but your eyes remain locked to mine across four thousand cubits of rolling hills. My chest lifts and falls like a newborn fawn. ⁴²The blue falls out of the sky. Creation is as empty as the day before time, and as endless. ⁴³God is hovering over us, a wind that tousles our hair, expanding. ⁴⁴I feel a great inhaling, everything I have ever known

draws inward, into God's deep inhaling. Floating, my feet are filled with air, and you keep looking at me. [45]I was a scroll sealed tightly in an earthen jar, hidden in a sheath of rock, and you have pierced me, unrolled me, and now you are reading me. [46]Your eyes are two disks filled with seeing. Jeremiah! [47]The light is vanishing, bleeding away from us. [48]My head is water, my eyes a fount of tears. [49]You look at me. Your eyes say, "Let there be," and all at once, I am.

> [50]And then you take a razor in your hand
> and sheer your lustrous locks. I lament!
> That I ever made such a vow!
> [51]The wind bears them onto the heights

and I gather them, every one, like a bundle of grain. [52]I tie them together with my arms. They fall over me in a swath of black silk. [53]You lower your eyes and the world reappears. [54]You might never look to me again, but it matters not. [55]I am cast into the depths, into the heartbeat of the sea. [56]Your sweetest floods engulf me and lovely breakers and billows sweep above me. [57]Your waters close in over me. I drink them in! I sink to the base of the mountains, rocking gently as a feather from a great height, weeds twine around my head, and I rest on the kelp of the ocean floor, soft and pure. [58]As many stars are in the Heavens is as many cubits deep am I, deep in love, drowning in dreaming.

# 8

All at once ~wrote Anatiya ~ my bones are seeped with understanding. [2]Were you the child who peeked into the room? [3]Suddenly the illusions of this life are torn out of their graves and exposed to the blazing sun. [4]All is layers, layers of meanings, existing together in the subtlest of harmony. [5]My ears are suddenly tuned in to these intricacies of music and meaning. [6]In this stationary rock I see a parade of activity. In the white core of the sun I see all colors. [7]I now hear your words, which I have loved from afar, which I have heard addressed always to others and never to me, I now hear them in layers. [8]I hear you speaking to me, almost courting, softly and tearfully, explaining to me, gently, the nature of being. [9]Do you love me? Have you always loved me? [10]On the surface you speak of the wicked folk, but underneath you tickle me with fantasies, with the voice of the bridegroom rejoicing over his bride.

[11]What you say to them they cannot interpret,
but I now see the myriad meanings
you heap upon the precious crown of the letter *yud*.
[12]I am now wise to the betrayal of sight!
[13]Eve saw that the fruit was a delight to the eyes,
and even so when she ate, her eyes were opened!
[14]There are so many layers to seeing,
the deepest of which is called insight.
[15]We are born with only the barest level of sight.
We are basically blind,
and ego is our stumbling block.
[16]I surrender my ego to loving you,
I surrender my being to love,
and at once my eyes are opened
and I see that we are naked,
and I see that we are alone
under a lush
canopy of trees
on a plush
carpet of dewy grass.
[17]Your fingers taste
sixty times sweeter than honey.
[18]Rivers wind through the whole land
and God's voice is here, strolling.
Fruit hangs with heavy pulp
sticky on our hands
and in our lips.
[19]Your lips are crimson.
Your body is gold
and seamless.
[20]A bed of blossoms
and beams of cedar
and cypress.
The flutter of a turtledove.
[21]My eyes are opened and I see

even deeper than Eve.
I see that I want to stay here,
I am not eager to leave.
<sup>22</sup>I love this clear-water wellspring.
I love this frankincense forest.
I have no trace of wanderlust.
<sup>23</sup>I spin the two cherubs
with their fiery swords
around and around
until they are dizzy
and giddy
and drunk on my rapture,
<sup>24</sup>so they think they are keeping us out,
but in truth they are keeping us in.

<sup>25</sup>I am wise to the deception of sight.
I see in this desert
there is the ghost of an ocean
<sup>26</sup>I see in this Temple
there is the Tower of Babel,
scratching at Heaven's
glassy surface.
<sup>27</sup>The House that bears His Name
is defiled to make a name for ourselves.
<sup>28</sup>God is pulling back His bow
like an archer.
His arrow is a foreign nation.
<sup>29</sup>He will scatter us soon
over the face of the earth.
He will confound our language
and confuse our tongue.
<sup>30</sup>I hear you weeping,
"All is not well."
<sup>31</sup>You know that we are naked and
only you and I are blushing.

[32]Only you and I are wise
to the flagrant bond between
shame
and joy.

~WROTE ANATIYA.

[33]I will not harvest the corners of our love

~WROTE ANATIYA

[34]but let the poor gather up grapes
and baskets of purple-hearted figs.
[35]I will toss morsels to the loveless throngs
as into a wishing well.
[36]Why do they sit by
with their heads bowed
and eyes lowered?
[37]Let them gather and search
for the fountain of youth
in the midst of the city,
and drink from its glistening draft.
[38]Sated in its dew
they will never die old,
but sing and dance into Sheol
a thousand years young.

[39]Lo, my kisses I will pile upon my palm like pollen on a petal,
and blow them to you on a sweet gust of my breath
that they might germinate in your pores.

~WROTE ANATIYA.

⁴⁰Your head is the chief cornerstone of the Temple
upon which bears down an unbearable wall.

⁴¹My heart is shattered when I see you crumble.
God's wrath is a poisoned well in your gut
rumbling up into your throat. Vile taste!
⁴²Where is our mikvah of pure living waters?

⁴³Hark! The outcry of my poor prophet!
The mountains tremble.
The Temple walls shudder and quake.
⁴⁴The world tilts awkwardly,
like a drunkard, staggering through the ruins.
⁴⁵Seized by desolation . . . I cry for you from the dark corner.
I gather your shadow into my arms.
⁴⁶It is brittle and cold, quaking in the first throes of dying.
⁴⁷I brush off the dust and kiss its fluttering eyelids,
and gently rock it in the cradle of my bosom, singing:
⁴⁸"Hush, shadow, hush. I am your island of calm.
Return to our prophet,
surround his body like a moat around a castle,
fed by the fount of his tears.
Let no killing thing cross.
Let none pull asunder."
⁴⁹The shadow slips from me, healed,
and Jeremiah finally succumbs
to slumber, ⁵⁰face damp,
and young as a child.
⁵¹In the morning I press my lips
to the tearstains on his sleeping mat,
and I shiver as a flower with pleasure
with the touch of morning dew.

# 9

O to be in the desert with you,
with its ribbons of gold and rose.
²To leave this people
and to hide in a secret oasis,
and to love unashamed
under the open sky

with its voyeuristic sun,
³our bodies sanded and rose-colored.
⁴The desert stares like the giant amber eye
of a lion, purring,
we dance and leap, two flecks,
where nobody heeds us

~WROTE ANATIYA.

⁵O friend of my heart,
were you only my brother
we could suckle from the same breast.
⁶We could speak loudly across the marketplace,
"Peace, sister! Peace, brother!"
⁷You could embrace me and kiss me lightly.
If only you were a nobody like me!
⁸If only you were insignificant, overlooked,
we could shout our careless love with trumpets
and none would pay us any heed!

~WROTE ANATIYA.

⁹I assure you, the place in my dreams does exist.
¹⁰A place on the opposite side of the world
that is the opposite of everything here.
¹¹A garden springs up in the midst of an orchard,
and a stone bench—

carved in the manner of Betzalel,
overlaid with gold,
two cherubs leaning in, wings touching
to form a seat for two—
waits by a fountain that spills,
whose bubbles are the giggling of children.
[12]The opposite of everything here,
the sandy road is a pathway of precious stones
crushed into glittering dust

~WROTE ANATIYA.

[13]Paradise is only as far as the flame from the wick.

[14]A bench in the manner of Betzalel
waits for two lovers to rest and find repose,
to gaze into each other's eyes
as into green pastures,
[15]while vines thick with roses entwine round their legs,
while their footprints fill with spring poppies
and lilies drop out of the sky.

[16]I know this place is called Milashuri,
and when we go there and grasp hands and find repose,
the spirit will move the cherub's wings
and lift the lovers over many ladders of cloud
upon the chariots of Amminadab.

[17]Dear Lord, in Your wisdom
You understand this girl,
whose life is but a forgotten dream,
whose heart is a shattered urn.
[18]Gather these pieces, merciful Lord!
Fit them into a mosaic on the Temple floor,
and let the high priests tread on my desire.
[19]I am but dust, my Lord.

Sweep me up!
Sweep me in Your kindness
into Divine Evermore!

[20]Jeremiah is being scolded on behalf of all people. God's words are fire-filled hailstones. [21]God gave His only daughter to Israel as a bride, and she has returned to Him bruised and mistreated. [22]Downcast and dejected, she frets about Heaven, twisting her porcelain hands. [23]"Don't avenge Yourself upon him, O Father, please! He is a good husband, with a pure love in his heart, I swear unto You! [24]He is just a bit young! A little stubborn, a little human, dear Father! Don't scatter him, don't slay him. [25]You can't expect him to be just like You!" [26]But God looks upon her and weeps. He says, "Once you had no creases on your brow, and your eyes were clear as a river." [27]He lifts up His sword to chase Israel. Torah falls to her knees and clutches His robe.

[28]She cries:
"It is only because I have become human in his arms!"
[29]She seizes the corner of His robe and it tears.
[30]He turns to her in anger and says:
"I have this day torn your marriage with Israel.
Summon the dirge-singers! [31]Let them wail for you.
From now on the sons of men shall not
take wives from among divine beings.
[32]My breath will not dwell in them forever."
Her tears wash over the mountain of the north.

[33]The sound of her wailing
is heard from Heaven.
[34]She clutches the golden ring
which Moses himself handed her
when she appeared to him
in blazing beauty.

[35]God is so jealous,
so livid when He looks at the hearts of men

that He forgets the redemptive love
found in the hearts of women!
And so I cry out, "I love!

"I love!

"I love!"

[36]My ears receive the teachings of Your mouth,
and yet, death creeps over my windowsill,
consuming the feathery hopes of young virgins
and of the frightened mothers with babes in their bellies and arms,
only because they stand innocently in Your barreling way
to cut off all the men from the squares.

[37]To punish You for tearing her marriage,
to punish You for pursuing her groom,
to punish You for the loves You left
piled like sheaves behind the reaper,
[38]Your daughter erases the names of the women from her scroll,
Your careful latticework of female legend she blots out, saying:
[39]"If You will not see us in Your wild stampede,
than I will not have You write us!"
[40]God is in search of man
and man is in search of God,
and woman is irreconcilably lost

~WROTE ANATIYA.

[41]You take note of the circumcised of Israel ~wrote Anatiya~ [42]You count
them with half shekels. When do you count me? [43]Am I the same as a forlorn girl of fourteen from Egypt or Edom, Ammon or Moab? [44]Who am
I in this great House of Israel? I will tell You who I am. [45]I am the Temple
treasure. I am the whisper of the secret name in the Holy of Holies. [46]I am
the quickened pulse. I am the blood that purifies the altar. [47]I am just as You
are, my God and my Redeemer, I am that I am. I will be what I will be.

## 10

Hear the words that I say to you, O mournful Jeremiah!

²Do not be dismayed by the portents in the sky, my love,
do not beat yourself over the profanity of others.
³You weary me with your sorrow,
weary me to death, my love,
every teardrop is a nail,
every sob is a hammer
that secures my grave.
Heaven forbid!
⁴You totter there like a scarecrow in a cucumber patch,
and the crows are getting wise to your impotence.
⁵Let them gorge themselves on the shallow minds,
and you walk away with me.
⁶I will kiss you until you are raw
and red and alive,
⁷I will kiss you until your senses sizzle
like sweet butter
on a hot stone.
You will see that it is good.

⁸You are hashmal, gleaming amber,
when streaking God-bolts
thrust jagged daggers across the sky,
slashing it into the slow-bleeding sunsets
that embrace your silhouette.
⁹You run but the storm never leaves you;
it clings like fog to a mountain.
¹⁰The lightning races fast as thought,
frantic for a place to land,
for a place to bridge sky and land
in a momentary star-way-stairway of light.
¹¹It leaves cedar and steppe unscathed,

preferring to pound its light into you,
my weary prophet,
striking with deafening light and blinding thunder.

[12]You are ignited and bright as hashmal;
you cage a tiny sun in your breast
and it streams through your eyes
and sears over your lips.
[13]I could be your blanket of snow;
I am as muted and blank.
I could quiet you and cool you.
[14]Your fever would melt me away
before my presence was felt.
A slight shiver is all I am.

[15]The world was created through a series of separations. Light from darkness. Day from night. Earth from sea from sky. Second from first.

[16]O, let my darkness reunite with his light!
Though the world be unborn,
though we return to the void,
[17]though we become unformed!
At least unformed we cannot bear Your yoke.
[18]Forgive me my mockery, dear God!
With what frivolity I speak,
with no discipline in my thoughts,
obscuring counsel without knowledge,
speaking without understanding
of things beyond me, which I do not know.
[19]I recant. I relent.
I am but dust and ashes!
[20]You established the world in Your wisdom.
[21]You bring forth the wind from Your treasuries.
[22]You form all things perfectly
and with purpose.

Mortal eyes cannot see this.

²³Dear God, how I love You!

How I love Your good Name!

²⁴You are my God and there is none else,

in the Heavens above and on the earth below,

all else is delusion.


²⁵I gather up my bundle from the ground

and march after my love like an ant.


²⁶For once, I am grateful for my muteness. When Jeremiah speaks, he is a masterful orator, expertly spinning lyrics and parables. ²⁷He harnesses his voice into speeches that dance before chariots of kings.


²⁸If I were to speak,

what folly would pour from my mouth!

²⁹I can blot out the words that I write

and pen them, inspired, anew.

³⁰But a spoken word cannot be retracted.

I may have broken cords, or

caused great commotion

if I spoke out of fever,

or out of distress.

³¹The passion in my soul

may have been dull when encased

in the limits of spoken language.

³²It is the spontaneity of speech

that frightens me the most!

Writing needs no such spontaneity.

³³How many times would I have opened my mouth

in a rush to call out, "How I need you! How it hurts!"

³⁴The shame! I can only imagine him

turning around,

shoulders dropping,

head shaking,

and then he would flee from my need,
from my intrusiveness,
from my noise.

<sup>35</sup>Or perhaps
he would fall to his knees,
perhaps my voice would shatter the spell
and free him, and he would weep into my neck,
my hands in his hair . . .
<sup>36</sup>I know, O Lord, that You have chosen this path for me,
and that it has meaning even without the spoken word.
<sup>37</sup>I know, also, that because my mouth is silent
my thoughts are all the louder.
You surely hear them. <sup>38</sup>You surely disapprove,
at times. But let me keep them.
Though they nag and disturb,
and become lusty and base.
<sup>39</sup>You may chastise me for them, O Lord, in measure.
<sup>40</sup>But let me keep them, lest I become naught,
as silent inside as out,
a numb thing,
with no self to keep herself company.

## 11

The covenant which Anatiya wrote ~

I make this covenant between you, Jeremiah son of Hilkiah, and my-self, Anatiya daughter of Avigayil, in the presence of the pink of dawn. <sup>2</sup>Because God has locked your soul in a golden cage, you cannot court and love a woman in the way of the common man. <sup>3</sup>(The common man does not know how fortunate he is!) <sup>4</sup>And so, I betroth myself to you in righteousness. I betroth myself to you for eternity. <sup>5</sup>As for you, I ask only one condition. <sup>6</sup>That you not let me die. <sup>7</sup>That you sustain me through the power of your calling from God. <sup>8</sup>And only when you are near the end of your days, that you allow my life to be released, that you let God in to gather me, and that you yourself, prophet, you yourself with your own hands take my body and carry me, wash me, and bury me in a white linen robe that you have worn. [9]You respond, "Amen."

[10]This is the covenant I make with you: [11]Though we may never touch in this life, though you may never know me, as the first man knew the first woman on the outskirts of paradise, I will bear for you offspring, indeed, as many as there are stars in the heavens. [12]However, the firstborn I shall not have to redeem, for the babe will not be the issue of my womb.

[13]Rather, we will adopt the unknowns. [14]We will adopt the children who feel a royalty in their breast, but have been given the role of the comedian. [15]We will adopt every mind who has a fantasy, for our love is none but a fantasy, a fantasy which infects, a fantasy as thick as this heat, a fantasy which draws the sweat from my body and leaves me short of breath. [16]We will be patriarch of vision, matriarch of dream.

[17]Every now and then, a person catches a glimpse of himself in a pool, and does not recognize his own face in the reflection. [18]Sometimes, a person does not recognize her entire life. In their minds, they are living another life. [19]A life of luxuries that never existed. A life of love that is never expressed. [20]A life of daring, a life that never surfaces, but is kept jailed inside by a name: daughter of, father of . . . or by a label: wife of, servant of. [21]Inside the merchant is a sailor. Inside the slave is a scribe. [22]Inside every person is a laughing, sprightly wish, an acrobat who swings from the clouds. [23]These will be our offspring, Jeremiah, every one.

[24]Some day, be sure, they will seize the gates of their foes.

[25]They will peel away the husks,
tired but determined.
[26]One day, be sure,
they will peck and push their way out of their shells,
roll into the light with their heads wobbling on little necks,
gasp air, blink,
and dry off,
[27]and suddenly,
every single one will come to be.
[28]The membrane that covers the world will dissolve,
and every one will be fantasy,
creative and chaotic,

spiraling upward in windstorms of color,
in chiming collisions.
²⁹On that day, the hosts of angels will look upon us
as a source of immeasurable joy.

³⁰This House is a dried cinder in a furnace, and I see there is a tremor
in the world. ³¹I see there is a pale terror that has settled on your face. ³²I
see in your eyes that it is coming, Jeremiah, a cold decree.

³³Remember in your despair that I am here.
³⁴I knead small cakes and roast a bit of meat
and leave it just inside your door.
³⁵I am for you a shawl,
draped limply over your shoulders,
with fringe worn with worry,
a comfort.
³⁶I have no part in their conspiracy.
They are only afraid of you
because you make them feel naked,
³⁷even the wealthy with their heavy garments
feel chilled and exposed in your presence.
³⁸They despise you because they are frightened.
³⁹But remember this name as you bemoan your loneliness:
Anatiya.
⁴⁰This is the name of the girl
whose love for you outweighs all hate.
⁴¹This is the name of the girl
whose love for you comes from the highest of truths.
I lay this love before you.

⁴²Assuredly, I hear them plotting, seeking your very life. They fear
your truth and figure to ensnare it like a dangerous beast. ⁴³They want to
kill the truth and continue making love with their lies and delusions. ⁴⁴I
am not afraid because God is a protective shield around you. ⁴⁵God will
break the teeth of your enemies and give them as prey to the jackals. ⁴⁶He
will incite death against them, and they will turn back, frustrated in their
designs. ⁴⁷Your refuge is in the Lord; you are His trusting servant.

## 12

How I admire my gutsy prophet!
You blame not the people but the God,
risking your own life to make this claim!
²He is the Maker of light and of darkness,
the Source of all good and evil.
³You rail and your words punch and puncture.
⁴A doubt is born in the highest heavens,
a reddish stain,
and the angels cower away from it in terror.
⁵They wonder why the Lord stands aloof
and heedless in times of trouble.
⁶If the ways of the wicked prosper,
is it not He who planted and sustained them?
⁷Their mouths are full of oaths, deceit, and fraud;
mischief and evil are under their tongues,
but did He not say, ⁸"Who gives man speech?
Who makes him dumb or deaf, seeing or blind?
Is it not I, the Lord?"
⁹Is this our God, Who commands us saying,
"From the fruit of the tree in the middle of the garden
you shall not eat, lest you die,"
¹⁰and then shows us a tree whose sensuality
is the very envy of life itself?
¹¹The wicked think, "God is not mindful.
He hides His face. He never looks!"
¹²The wicked think God does not see them
lurking in covert places,
spying out the hapless.
You do see them, God!
¹³How long will you give the enemy the upper hand?
¹⁴How long will the land languish
while the adversaries gloat
in treacherous decadence?

[15]The Holy One answers you;
"If you race with the foot-runners and they exhaust you,
How then can you compete with the horses?"
[16]You see only what is before you,
like a horse wearing blinders,
[17]while I see from the beginning to the end in a blink.
I cause the rain to come in its season.

[18]See now, Jeremiah prepares his case,
though he knows God will win it.
[19]His challenge is barely audible,
and yet it crashes through firmaments.
[20]It re-releases the hurtled accusations
of that victim Job:
[21]"Will You harass a driven leaf?
Will You pursue dried up straw
that You decree for me bitter things,
and put my feet in stocks?
[22]I am like a garment eaten by moths.
[23]Man born of woman is short-lived and sated with trouble.
[24]He blossoms like a flower and withers.
He vanishes like a shadow
and does not endure.
[25]Why do You fix Your gaze on such a one as me?"

[26]Who can produce a clean thing out of an unclean one?
No one!
[27]And You have made me unclean!
You molded my clay with silt on Your hands.

[28]You set the limits that man cannot pass.
[29]Turn away from me! That I may be at ease until,
like a hireling, I finish out my day.
[30]O, leave me alone, You unbearable weight!
If You would leave me alone,

if You would just let me be,
³¹I would console the bereaved,
I would clothe the naked,
yes, I would marry the orphan.
³²But You cage me
as a hostage in Your wrath!

³³As water wears away stone,
torrents wash away earth,
so You destroy man's hope.
³⁴You overpower him forever and he perishes.
³⁵He may well slay me.
I may have no hope,
Yet I will argue my case before Him.
³⁶Your hands shaped and fashioned me
and then destroyed every part of me.

³⁷Thus wrote Anatiya: Give him to me, O God!—before You whittle him away into nothing, ³⁸before You chisel him narrower and narrower and chip away his defenses and leave him brittle as exposed bone. ³⁹Dear God, I love his flesh and his heart. I love the waves of silk that grow from his scalp. ⁴⁰I love the pink pads of his fingertips. I love the rapid pulse in his neck. I love the perfect arch of his sole, the hollow behind his knee, the breath he heaves at day's end. ⁴¹Give him over to me, O God! I will cherish his humanity. ⁴²I will soothe the flesh and blood of him. ⁴³Perhaps You will terrify and torment the soul of Jeremiah for all eternity with Your whims. What impact have I on Your eternity? ⁴⁴But for these fewscore years, while he is housed in a tender, bristling shell that ages and shivers and aches, give him to me... ⁴⁵because I love him. I love him, not for what he can do for Heaven or for Israel. ⁴⁶I love him because I am Anatiya and he is Jeremiah. ⁴⁷Let go of Him, Father. Here am I, a frail, female mortal, laughably commanding You the Commander: ⁴⁸You shall not murder, love.

## 13

You are in your room unfolding a swath of linen. ²I peek at you through the cracks in the lattice. My heart is pounding and aching. ³Perhaps I am one of the wicked ones! Lurking here in the covert places, spying on you in the sanctity of your own place. ⁴Somehow I feel I have the right to trail you in the open squares, to scrutinize the details of your gestures. ⁵Even when I watch you sleep, I do not feel too invasive, for I know you are really in some far and secret place. ⁶But as I watch you now, awake in your room, engaged in an act so simple and domestic, I want to cry. ⁷Do you sense that you are not alone? Or have you been so long under the watchful eye of our God that you have lost your sense of privacy? ⁸I don't want to rob you! I don't want to steal your respite of solitude. ⁹I only ever wanted to give to you, just give, but I can't tear myself away. ¹⁰My nails dig into the ledge, and my eyes rake you, greedily sapping your life. ¹¹O God, I do not want this, I do not want to peep into windows like an alley cat. ¹²My eyes are burning. My mouth is dry. The palms of my hands are sweating.

¹³You take off your robe and stand naked. ¹⁴My tongue cleaves to the roof of my mouth. ¹⁵My bones are seized with a violent trembling. ¹⁶Here is my prophet, husband of my soul.

¹⁷A luminance emanates from your skin.
Your thighs are smooth as the shore.
Your belly is an ivory tablet.
¹⁸You stretch your arms to the ceiling,
and the whole length of you is ignited like sunlight
striking a tall waterfall.
¹⁹You walk, in the dappled light,
mussing your hair with your fingers.
²⁰Your body gleams like the skin of a dolphin
and you move through the air as through water,
every muscle a dancer.
²¹And the covenant in your lap is a delight to the eyes,
let my eyes fall out! My last image . . .

²²You touch yourself, lightly, with the linen, as you wrap it around your loins. You wrap it around snugly, just as God told you. ²³Your chest rises and falls. You breathe easily here, alone in your room. ²⁴My face is shining with oil. My hands are dripping with myrrh. ²⁵I begin to sob heavily at the sight of your beauty. ²⁶I fall back against the wall and sink down, my chest heaving. ²⁷You emerge from your door fully clothed and head out on the road to Perath to bury the loincloth, as God has commanded you. ²⁸I cannot follow. I am breathless and faint.

²⁹I miss my mother. ³⁰Thief! Give me back my dozen and one, give me that age before You stole her breath and stole my voice. ³¹I want to run away before I lose control, before I leap over him in his sleep like Ruth on the threshing floor. ³²There is a boulder in my head, so heavy, so tired. I crawl into a corner and sleep, it seems, for a long, long while. ³³When I wake there are fresh tears on my face. ³⁴My mouth is moving, tongue-twisted, I am babbling to myself, and if I could hear it, it would be nothing but a baby's nonsense. ³⁵I saw your nakedness and I am left in a spin. ³⁶Utterly dazed. Jeremiah, I am a child! You mustn't overwhelm me so!

³⁷Some time later you go again to Perath
and I gather the strength now to follow.
There you kneel on the earth
and scratch up the soil in your cupped palms.
³⁸You unbury the linen loincloth,
as God had commanded you.
It is ruined and eaten away.
³⁹The loincloth is God's metaphor
for Judah and Jerusalem,

but for me,
it is no metaphor at all.
⁴⁰It is a real buried treasure,
a valuable diadem.
It embraced you around your thighs.
⁴¹You leave it by the wayside as you return to your home.
⁴²I gather it up and tuck it into my dress.
⁴³I wash it delicately in the Jordan river.

⁴⁴I immerse it three times like a holy instrument.
Scrub it lightly with a stone.
Soon it returns to its linen white.
⁴⁵I squeeze out the water over my face.
O, endless spring day!
⁴⁶I sew the holes,
repair the hem,
and embroider in rainbow threads the words,
⁴⁷"God's blessing on Jeremiah and Anatiya."
⁴⁸I lift up my skirts
and tie it as a sash around my waist.
It binds us together, my love.

⁴⁹A camel cannot change his humps
nor a leopard change his spots.
Just so, I cannot abandon the chase
when I am so practiced a stalker!
⁵⁰And so I will continue to shadow my prophet
and daily take measured portions of you,
like an ailing woman takes her medicines.
⁵¹A spoonful of your teaching,
a cupful of your dreams,
a handful of your yearning,
a mouthful of your tears.

~WROTE ANATIYA.

⁵²At night
I lift my skirts and untie the linen.
⁵³I fold it the way a priest folds his holy garment
and lays it by his head while he sleeps.

## 14

The words which Anatiya wrote concerning the drought.

²Judah is gasping for breath,
wheezing like new widow
who has run out of tears.
³Salt covers the rocks like a fungus,
evidence of a century of crying.
Her grassy fields are crackling chaff.
⁴I return to my once-verdant trees on the hillside.
They are hunched and beaten.
⁵I spit onto the ground at their base
but the ground just refuses my water.
⁶What have you done
but be canopies of shade?
What have you done
but freshen the stale air,
that you should be shamed and humiliated like this?
⁷I was once your woodsy fairy,
running and leaping through your branches,
which craned to graze my shoulders,
to touch my motion,
know my love.
⁸I was once your green princess,
dancing about with the hind of dawn,
with psalms of praise on our lips.
⁹Once you wore emerald robes
that breathed in the gentlest wind.
¹⁰Now you are pillars of dust.
I cover my head in sorrow.

¹¹And the people are such hypocrites,
agonizing over the souring crops,
pouting and pleading

while pointing an accusatory finger.
¹²"Why are You like a stranger in the land,
like a man who is stunned?"
they whine to God.
¹³Hypocrites! Without their bread and their flowers
they are suddenly filled with awe for God,
with pious resentment
that the Hand should withhold.
¹⁴In their pleading is a berating tone,
emasculating God with their chiding:
¹⁵"Why are You like a man who is stunned,
like a warrior who cannot give victory?"
¹⁶And God thinks hotly, "Why am I stunned?
Why am I stunned?
¹⁷I am stunned by your arrogance!
I am stunned by your gall!
¹⁸Without your good harvest you suddenly need Me,
but the moment I replenish your bread and your flowers,
you race to the beds of your prostitutes and no-gods!
¹⁹And as for your question, 'Why are You like a man?'
I will tell you.
²⁰The less like Me you behave,
the more like you I become."

²¹Thus wrote Anatiya concerning Jeremiah: How different is Jeremiah from that king of old, Samson! ²²Samson was a brute and Jeremiah is a sage. Samson stood with his hands outstretched upon the pillars that supported the temple of Dagon. ²³Jeremiah stands with his hands outstretched upon the pillars that support the world: Justice and Mercy.

²⁴Samson stood there full of rage, eyes gouged out and blood-crusted. ²⁵Samson raised his voice in prayer, that he might have just one final moment of glory, end his life in one final, extravagant massacre. ²⁶He measured his success by small moments of great satisfaction, be it in the arms of a skilled lover, or in the death of a Philistine town.

²⁷Jeremiah stands there full of love, a love that tortures you (how much easier it would be to hate!), eyes blinded with a thin white film of

suffering. [28]Jeremiah raises his voice in prayer, that he might remind God of eternity. [29]He demonstrates the patience of the sea, lapping at the foot of a mountain as he appeals to God's everlasting kindness.

[30]Samson pulled the pillars down and the temple crashed upon all the lords and people feasting in it. [31]Jeremiah holds the pillars up, with thin fingers and white knuckles, and pressed lips, and gripping toes, and all the might in his reed-like body. I love you, Jeremiah. [32]You would answer Samson's riddle differently. [33]Samson asked, "Out of the eater came something to eat, out of the strong came something sweet." The Philistines answered "honey" and "lion," rightly so in the simplest way. [34]But I know what Jeremiah would say:

Out of the eater came something to eat,
out of the strong came something sweet
[35]means that out of God's strong wrath
comes our sweet redemption.
God's wrath is the eater,
it consumes and destroys.
[36]Out of God's wrath comes the need to repent,
which hastens the coming of redemption.
[37]Redemption is the ultimate fulfillment,
pure nourishment for the hearty appetite
of the soul. [38]Won't You feed us, Father?
Won't You powder our landscape with manna?
[39]Won't You give us something sweet to eat
instead of choking us with Your bitter Truth?

[40]The people refuse to believe
that God has rejected them.
[41]They crane their necks to the skies,
smacking their dry tongues on their palates
like baby birds whose mother does not return.
[42]They see now that they have nothing to give,
nothing to offer up to God,
no good deed, no small kindness,
for they have been utterly spent

in the chambers of foreign gods.
⁴³Their fingers are so dirty,
they could not even touch a child's lips
without spreading contagion,
let alone offer up offerings to God.
⁴⁴And so they say,
"Do it for Your name's sake!"
Save us for Your Own peace of mind,
because our lives are nothing.
⁴⁵"Do not dishonor Your glorious throne!"
⁴⁶Rescue us for Your sake,
not for ours, for we have no merit.
⁴⁷We only have to live with our sins for
one hundred years.
But You live with Your grievance forever.

## 15

Do you remember the days when the word of the Lord was rare? ²The
prophets and priests could sleep at night in their comfortable nooks. ³In
those days, their heads were fuzzy with pleasant dreams and the halls of
the temple at Shiloh echoed with contented snoring, until the voice of
young Samuel cried out, "I'm coming!" and woke the drowsy priest. ⁴But
the people today are so steeped in illusion, no charge could revive them.
⁵No broken tablets could make them repent.

⁶It has already been determined:
Who will die by fire,
and who will die by drowning.
⁷Who will die by hunger or thirst,
and who will die slowly,
over many generations in captivity.

⁷My pen blasphemes without my consent! Black ink in the eyes of King
Menasseh, who turned the croplands into a valley of salt. ⁸He set up a
forest of sacred posts throughout the city, dead things jutting out of the

ground with mocking faces. ⁹How the living trees recoil! He made idols
as plentiful as dust and tweaked at their wooden breasts.

¹⁰The only time I recall seeing my father cry
was when he told the story of his visit
to the valley at the foot of Jerusalem.
He cast off his sandals

~WROTE ANATIYA


¹¹and rolled his eyes backwards.
¹²He had been elated to see King Menasseh
escorted in royal entourage
toward the center of the valley.
¹³With two cawing chickens in his right hand
and a goat by the beard in his left,
my father scrambled up a scoping rock.
¹⁴He saw the sovereign clasp his son
and kiss his lips. ¹⁵The king's forehead
was burning red with zealotry,
his mouth clenched in an
anxious, impassioned grin.
¹⁶Then my father noticed
the little prince's wrists
bound in silk cords.
¹⁷The king laid the boy upon a stony ramp,
and kicked him mightily
so that he rolled, yelping, to the furnace,
and while the fire belched
¹⁸the people flagellated themselves in worship,
lifting their arms
and dancing,
and the king broke into an ecstatic sweat

~WROTE ANATIYA.

<sup>19</sup>Woe is me, my father, that he should be so pitiful—
A man of conflict and strife with himself!
<sup>20</sup>After being catastrophe's witness,
instead of throwing his arms around his only child,
he narrowed his eyes and cursed me.

> <sup>21</sup>Anatiya said:
> I am the remnant of Israel,
> clinging to the sacred curtain
> like a burr.
> <sup>22</sup>Though the slaughterer emerges
> from the shadows
> on the north side of the altar,
> I will not let go.
> I am hooked into the weave.

<sup>23</sup>I have seen the morning priests
slay their victim swiftly
through the nape.
<sup>24</sup>O to be that docile lamb
led to the slaughter unaware!
<sup>25</sup>Better to be the women, the children,
the lame and the sick, the stragglers
who were cut down by Amalek
before any fear could surface.
<sup>26</sup>Better contented absent-mindedness
than this slow-killing thing
wielding its sword
like an elusive sunbeam
under our chins.

<sup>27</sup>O Lord, You know—
Remember Jeremiah, and take thought of me.
<sup>28</sup>I see Jeremiah's fear shifting in tide
from troubled concern for the inhabitants of this city

and their inevitable doom
to a darting-eye paranoia
and frozen sorrow.
[29]"Don't take me away!"
The pain of my prophet
when all nuance and lyric are shed,
is simple, a clean stabbing of loneliness.
[30]"Don't let me perish!" before I experience
a single smile or one pleasured sigh in this life,
he begs.
[31]He is not silent like Moses in the bulrushes,
no, he cries
like the abandoned babe
Ishmael, whose wailing was heard
in the highest heavens. [32]O God!
Your name is a manacle fastened to him!
[33]More bearable the wood on Isaac's back
than the Hand You push down on him,
a millstone grinding his sweetest head,
his most beautiful head. [34]Leave him be,
dear God! Leave him be!
So?
Let him make merry and die in drunken stupor.
[35]Why must his pain be endless?
Why must his wound be incurable?
Why must his soul be parched
of love and delight?

[36]Had I only a vial of Hezekiah's tears
and a cake of figs
I could cure him of mortality.
[37]I could buy him a jubilee
of berries and streams
and pillows of cloud
upon which to lay his heavy dreams.

³⁸One day the people will run to you
like pups to their master when he comes home . . .
Come home Jeremiah

~WROTE ANATIYA.

³⁹Let him come home into the hands of quiet.
Let him come home into the clutches of calm.

# 16

The words of Anatiya:
If God said to you as He said to Hosea, "Take a wife of harlotry," I would
stand at the entrance to Enaim, but I would not cover my face with a veil.
²I would wait with my face shining and exposed, and I would not ask,
"What will you pay for sleeping with me?" ³I would accept no pledge, but
give myself freely. I would walk through the town of Gibeah alone before
dawn. ⁴I would skip through the squares of Sodom and Gomorrah. ⁵I
would bathe naked on rooftops in the noonday sun in view of the king's
palace. ⁶I would lower crimson ladders from my window. ⁷I would make
my name more known than Gomer or Rahab. ⁸If only to be your wife. If
only to bear you Children-of-the-Living-God.
    ⁹For thus says Anatiya:

Do not mourn the metamorphosis of a holy people.
¹⁰What appears as sin is only sleep,
the sleep of a caterpillar molting within its damp cocoon

~WROTE ANATIYA.

¹¹With patience and wisdom
a winged creature will emerge.
¹²Graves will open and new eyes will
blink away tears in the redeeming light,
and rise, with four gossamer wings
that flutter and stretch,
a celebration of flight

and birth. [13]And Jerusalem
will spin slowly as a great wheel
rising above the mountain,
our spirits contained within it.

[14]At that time, Jeremiah, I am going to stand from my place. [15]I am
going to ascend before your eyes, and your ears will be filled with the
sound of mirth and gladness. [16]And your voice shall be the rejoicing of
the bridegroom, lifted in song. [17]And my voice shall shake off its yoke of
silence, and carol you, with the perfumed tones of the happiest bride.

[18]Assuredly, a time is coming ~ wrote Anatiya ~ when the two stones
on Aaron's vestments will crumble, and weight will be lifted, and there
will be no need for memory. [19]A time is coming when half a world will
not be balanced on each of my prophet's shoulders, bearing him down.
[20]But rather, the world will bear him up. [21]He will stand upon the world,
Elijah's right arm hooked around his waist, and I will be there, curled in
my prophet's palm, sucking his thumb like a baby.

[22]Lo, the nets that sweep the sea

~WROTE ANATIYA

shall sift the desert sand.
[23]The righteous will slip through,
lean as parchment,
and the wicked ones with hearts of stone
will be swept up to the place of judgment.
There is no hiding.
[24]And do not be stunned.
Do not dare say you had no warning.
[25]Jeremiah is there preaching
with strained and hoarse voice.
Listen to him!
[26]Run from your evil paths
and hide from your iniquitous desire,
lest you be tossed into the ocean

with iron-clamped shoes.
²⁷My heart is in shreds
when they dismiss your shaken plea
as if it were nothing,
as if it were lunacy.
²⁸I want to shout:
Hear him, O Israel!
Jeremiah is your prophet
ordained by your God!
²⁹You chit-chat with the buck-toothed gods
you have made for yourselves,
and utterly disregard
God's own spokesman.
³⁰Have you forgotten the very name of your God?

## 17

Someday someone will uncover
these, my words inscribed,
and my name her lips will murmur,
summoning up my sleepy spirit.
²And my spirit will not frighten her,
nor cause her to shy away,
but draw her close.
³She, the reader, will wonder aloud to me
whether such a love could be,
whether it is possible to be
so pent up with poetry
and yet invisible to the object
of deep adoration.
⁴Slow death,
slow seeping of life, she will say,
how do you endure it?
⁵And I say: But for her do I endure this pain.
But for her do I live,

my distant and unknown reader
who is closer and more intimate with my heart
than any other in this world.
⁶For I believe with perfect faith that she will release me,
that she will speak me,
resurrect me and save me.
⁷You save me, beautiful reader,
and my story, from centuries of suffocation.
⁸And I, in turn, perhaps,
give to you,
by not extinguishing the power of this love from the world,
by not taking my life, despite its crushing burden.
⁹We must live and record, brilliant interpreter,
lest the libraries be stacked with scrolls of war
and not one leaf of love.


¹⁰Thus writes Anatiya:
I cannot let you out of my sight.
¹¹Your flesh is white-hot and fine gold.
I want to sear my body against it.
¹²My thoughts turn from all that is holy.
I want to ravage you like Ruth on the threshing floor.
¹³I want to lie at your feet while you sleep.
There is a hailstorm pounding at my breast.
¹⁴I want to be under you, over you,
braid my legs through yours. I run to the wilderness
seeking shelter from my storm.
¹⁵I want to bite into you,
tug at your hair in clumps,
beat that vicious God out of you,
thresh out intrusive visions
and leave only skin and pulse and want.
¹⁶I fall to my knees before a stream's muddy bank
and choke on tears as hard as diamonds.

[17]I scratch into my arms with my nails.
My eyes are hot coals, my eyes,
my mouth, my nose are running,
gasping, death is upon me, this heat . . .
[18]O God, how shameful am I!

[19]What sort of madness is in me,
strangles me, that
I straddle a smooth rock,
my face in the mud, my mouth
sputtering and gasping your name.

[20]I lay in the water and the stream rushes over me,
smoothing my hair, loosening the mud from my dress,
the filth from my skirts. [21]Clear water, clear sky,
clear and cold mind, numbing, icy,
the sky is darkening,
translucent cobalt,
chilly stars, I will freeze here this night
in this watery shrine,
freeze this desire from my heart.
[22]Angels, come! Pluck out the black from my heart.
Wash me in snow and in mist,
Fount of living waters.

[23]Heal me, O Lord, and let me be healed.
Save me, and let me be saved.
[24]I am asking you nicely. So nicely.
So peacefully, letting go.
[25]The water is rising over my eyes.
It is better this way, no tears.
[26]It slides up my chest, leaps over the loop
of my neck and my chin, laughing,
into my mouth, cold and clear.
[27]My toes and fingers, cold and blue,

and lips, numb, teeth clicking.
[28]Freeze me, preserve me, that this fire doesn't leap up
and consume the world in holocaust. [29]Freeze me.
The sky is dark. I will sleep here, come what may.
[30]If I die, submerged in grasses and pebbles and little frogs,
let it be. [31]If I wake, let me be clean
and clear.
[32]Come sleep, come slumber,
come ministering angels and watchers of the night.
[33]I do not long for the fatal day,
but I do long for the day after.

The waking day.

[34]The Lord commands Jeremiah to stand by the People's Gate, by which the kings of Judah enter and by which they go forth, and by all of the gates of Jerusalem. [35]He is the town crier. His voice is his bell rippling through the stale air. [36]To the passersby he seems another merchant crying his wares. [37]But the people prefer to purchase a scoop of flour or swatch of cloth for half a shekel, than to hear his word for nothing.
[38]I nestle between a limestone wall and a sack of grain listening and shivering. [39]I woke before dawn on the bank of the stream with a coldness that reached the very heart of me. [40]I heard looters not far from me, crouching in the brushes and counting the stolen goods they had amassed. [41]I feared for my life lest they find me. With the sun, they moved on and I stole over the edge to watch them go. [42]A pair of ugly, angular, wiry men, and I thought, "Two more cinders for your fire, dear God." [43]I hurried to the city, my wet sandals cutting into my ankles. [44]I searched each gate in turn until I found you standing tall and beaming and I nestled myself here. The merchants are busy and the Sabbath is as any other day to them.
[45]I am cold. Would you, if you knew that my illness grew worse, take me to the upper chambers and lay me down upon my own bed? [46]Would you stretch out over me three times and revive me? Build a fire, ignite candles, cup my face in your warm hands, and breathe over me with your rosemary breath? [47]I am cold and my head hurts as if a ring of ice is closing around it. And there you stand, through my haze, man of miracles. [48]Your mouth is moving, saying, "Carry no burdens through the gates of

Jerusalem on the Sabbath day," while your eyes see the people hunched under their burdens, their deliveries and merchandise. ⁴⁹I see the gates suddenly catch fire, flames leaping over the top. The heat is immense. ⁵⁰The water trapped in the stones of the great gate boil and they explode, lodging into skin. ⁵¹The people are caught up in a frantic running and the fire spreads instantaneously around the walls of the city, and one by one the gates cave in. ⁵²I uncover my eyes and it is all as it was. Soft sunlight and bustling people thinking average thoughts. ⁵³Do we share the same loathsome premonitions, my dear? I see that we do. ⁵⁴I see from your eyes that the stones tell you things you do not want to know.

## 18

I followed my love to the house of a potter. He tucked his robes underneath and sat at the potter's feet. ²I hesitated outside the door. Would it be suspicious if I were to enter? Just another young toiler seeking respite in the soft whooshing of the potter's wheel. ³I entered and kneeled by the potter's left side, across from my love. ⁴Jeremiah gazed intently at the potter's hands. His fingers pinched and smoothed the clay, and if the vessel he was making was spoiled, he would make it into another. ⁵O, that people could be so malleable in Your hands and not so stiff-necked! ⁶But God cannot deal with us as this potter deals with clay, for the artist has no claim over his creation once it leaves his hands.

⁷The word of the potter came to us: "Any vessel begins with an empty space. You see, first there is the presence of a void, and it is the duty of the potter to contain that void. ⁸Look now." The potter cupped the void just over his wheel. ⁹He said, "Sometimes I find here a masculine void, round and full, with a narrow neck from which to pour. A private void, one that wants to be contained in darkness and not exposed. ¹⁰But this moment, this moment I find a feminine void." The potter swept his hands under the space in a large bowl-shape. ¹¹"An open void, one that receives that which is poured.

¹²"If you have no respect for the void and its immense power," the potter revealed to us, "then you cannot understand." ¹³Jeremiah bowed his head and whispered, "I understand . . . that the breath of God is in man before he is ever formed from the clay."

¹⁴Assuredly, thus writes Anatiya:
We watched the potter all afternoon.
Dappled light danced in from the window,
¹⁵as if it were so natural for little me
to sit in the same room as a prophet of God,
perfectly still as a mountain rock,
watching him watch.
¹⁶His eyes are pools of Lebanon snow.
I see in them an imperfect reflection of the potter's hands.
¹⁷God is showing him a vision. The hands,
in his eyes, are light and not flesh.
The clay, in his eyes,
is a temple, not a jug,
razed and erected and razed again.
¹⁸The pieces are swept away like a plague of locusts
in a strong east wind.
¹⁹This close to you,
I feel my mind dropping in dry crumbles
down a long waterless well.
²⁰I hear the hollow echoing
as I fall away.

²¹Outside they are devising a plot against Jeremiah, lashing at him with lizard tongues. ²²They are eager to wall up his words with cedar wood and silver battlements so as not to be harassed by his warnings and pleading.

²³Is it worth it, O Jeremiah,
is it worth it for you,
these long years in the pit
while your brethren merrily break bread?
²⁴Was it worth it, O Job,
the holocaust of your children
and the eruption of your skin,
was it worth it to sit, lacerated,

on a pile of ash and scrapings of dead skin
<sup>25</sup>for the reward of fourteen thousand sheep,
six thousand camels,
one thousand yoke of oxen,
one thousand she-asses,
and ten shiny new children to call your own?
<sup>26</sup>Is it worth it, O Lord,
this famine and bereavement,
this death and wailing,
for the reward of a new covenant,
a new heaven and new earth?

## 19

But here in this room, with its fresh, wet air, the potter tousles Jeremiah's hair, smoothes his locks black as raven feathers. <sup>2</sup>Jeremiah leaves with a heavy earthen jug under his arm. <sup>3</sup>I rush and press my face into the potter's hand that touched him, and I burst into sobbing. <sup>4</sup>He hushes and holds me. He feels my fever in his hand. <sup>5</sup>He lays me in a vat of cool clay, covered with a thin drapery, where I sleep, drenched and shivering and healing. <sup>6</sup>When I wake I kiss his hands again, potter-healer. <sup>7</sup>I see him in a vision all at once, in a colorful hanging garden in Babylon, wise, healthy, faraway. <sup>8</sup>I leave my body's impression in the vat of clay, but I take my void with me.

<sup>9</sup>Jeremiah smashed that belly-round jug in the sight of all the men. In the wake of its silence <sup>10</sup>he charged, "So will God smash this people and this city, as one smashes a potter's vessel, which can never be mended." <sup>11</sup>I watch the clay-chips shatter and I think about the years. Years that can never be restored. <sup>12</sup>I am no girl anymore. These hips could bear children and these breasts could nurse them. <sup>13</sup>This skin is swarthier and these hands are coarser. <sup>14</sup>I compare myself to the other maidens of the land. I have all of my teeth, and my hair is thick and long, soft and unbroken. I keep my nails clean. I am growing into a fine, strong woman. <sup>15</sup>Yet all of this beauty shall remain dusty and untouched, nard whose perfume will never spread. <sup>16</sup>No scented ointment will be sprinkled over this head. Unpampered, untouched, but not wasted. <sup>17</sup>I love you, Jeremiah. I care not

about the metaphor of the shattered jug. I worry only that the shards not cut your lovely feet.

¹⁸At twilight, Jeremiah rests by a rock. His eyes close and I see he is sleeping. ¹⁹Blessed are You, for the gift of sound sleep. ²⁰I scurry in the withdrawing light to gather up the pieces of the jug. I wrap them into a bundle. ²¹In the world to come, dear God, while You are restoring living spirits to the dead, if it is not too much trouble, I pray You mend this little jug. It is most precious to me.

## 20

The day the moon fell out of the sky and killed me.

²That winter pale, sun-white skin that I traced every moment with feathery thoughts, they gripped and bruised. ³They beat him, heaven help him! about his golden head and silken raven locks, with the wooden clubs of the most brutish hunters, they flogged him and battered even the soles of his feet that I would kiss, ⁴that I would wash with my hair and spring water, his ivory chest they flogged, God! don't abandon him, ⁵the most kind, the most frightened little wonder-eyed child of a man, You, his shield, help him! ⁶pursue them and break out their teeth those that jab and attack and drag him coughing and shocked, crumpled into himself.

⁷I threw myself at the feet of Pashhur son of Immer, chief officer of the House of the Lord, and clutched his robes and begged, screaming, ⁸"Stone me to death! I have blasphemed in my thoughts. I have lusted after a true prophet of the Lord. Stone me to death that I not see them terrorize him so!" ⁹But he shook me off, frightened by my gaping mouth which gasped but made no sound, by my eyes that burned. ¹⁰For one day they locked him in a cell at the Upper Benjamin Gate in the House of the Lord. I sat in Benjamin Gate all night, wide-eyed awake. ¹¹I could feel his presence above me, through the rock, slumped onto the floor of his cell. ¹²I could feel the rhythmic pulsing of his welts and bruises, and the dull pain that washed over him like the surf lapping over the white shore. ¹³I watched the constellations roll over the dark sky, distant and sure. ¹⁴Some day we too, darling, will slide across the sapphire pavement, two graceful, long-necked cranes skimming the waters. ¹⁴This day I feel myself aging. ¹⁵This day I want so much to hate the men who flogged you, but I can only love, more deeply, more purely. ¹⁶Know, Jeremiah, how much joy for you

is in me. How I serve you adoringly, and on account of you, your God I
do forgive.

[16]To love a prophet
is to be utterly rejected,
a constant laughingstock
at whom everyone jeers.
[17]For he knows you are trailing behind him.
Everything is revealed to him
and though you are naked to his vision,
you are invisible to his eyes.
[18]He sees through the raging fire in your heart
with cooling clarity and leaves you helpless and dejected
with a humiliation for all time.
[19]But if you say "I will not think of him,
no more will I speak his name,"
his name reverberates off of your bones
[20]and your sinews are taught as Esau's bow,
you quiver with no release
until you feel you are in the very throes of death.
[21]To love a prophet
is to be utterly fulfilled,
knowing you are this close to Vision,
this near to Voice,
[22]and no fire comes forth to consume you
and no angel descends to strike you.
You feel radiant emanations
of the God that is in him
[23]and it amazes you,
that only you, among all people with names of renown,
should gain entrance into God's inner chamber,
[24]that your love should fit so snugly into that lock,
that hosts of angels should sympathize with you
and divine beings sustain you
[25]when you have no shekel to even purchase a morsel of bread,

that you, dark and comely and untended,
should be here, perched on the edge of Solomon's couch.

²⁶If I could dig up the body of Elisha,
I would touch you with one of his bones like a wand
and bring you back to life,
to a life that I know must exist,
²⁷where tides are even-tempered
and sunlight citrus-sweet.
²⁸Let me rinse your worn-out soul
in the warm fountains of the Galil
that bubble up from hidden springs
so that you emerge, ²⁹your lips
blessing the day you were born,
praising the man
who brought your father the news
that a boy was born to him,
and gave him such joy!
³⁰If God only would do for you
what He did for wicked Balaam,
and turn your curses into blessings,
³¹and turn your multitude of enemies into
pinpoints of light that guide ships and nations
³²and let us spend all our days in love,
in the coy pastels of early morning.

## 21

I followed Pashhur son of Malchiah and Zephaniah son of Maaseiah after they begged of you to inquire of God on behalf of King Zedekiah.
²Everyone knows in what high regard Heaven holds you. ³"Put in a
good word for us," they urged. "Coax out of God a wonder so that King
Nebuchadrezzar of Babylon will withdraw his armies from us."

⁴I followed the messengers to the palace after you assured them that
God Himself would battle against Zion with anger and rage and great
wrath, after you assured them that all hope is lost, that their families would

die of sword, pestilence, or famine. ⁵I followed them after you terrified them. They walked slowly. Feet dragging long troughs in the sand. Faces pale and hair blazing white in the sun. ⁶They were discussing poisonous roots, and whether they should take some rather than bear these grim tidings to the king. ⁷"The king could dismiss Jeremiah's words. He could dismiss them as resentment for having been flogged." ⁸"We could hide, God knows, perhaps some cave in the Negev and wait for the storm to pass . . ." ⁹and after a heavy sigh, "O, my sons, my sons!" ¹⁰"We shall take the root presently. Pass through our homes and instruct our sons once more, and then go off as friends, you and I, with this message sealed in our hearts by dead lips." ¹¹"He will kill us, I am sure." "Who?" "The King." ¹²"Which one?"

¹³Pashhur and Zephaniah ascended the stairway to the summit of the wall, nodding solemnly at the guard. ¹⁴I am behind them, riding their shadows. ¹⁵They sat with their legs draped over the edge like two boys at a spring. ¹⁶We could see the encampments of Babylonian troops sprawled out, the sun glinting playfully off their metal. ¹⁷The aging priests snapped the root, over which grew a fine flaking fungus, between them. ¹⁸They rolled the root between their fingers, considering it. ¹⁹The son of Malchiah turned to me and said, "Dear woman, go and tell the prophet Jeremiah that we delivered his message safely to the King." ²⁰The son of Maaseiah added solemnly, "To the King Who rules heaven and earth."

²¹They lifted the root to their mouths and I darted toward them, with the instinct of a hornet diving to the sting with no regard for its own death. ²²My two hands flung out and I snatched both roots out of their hands before they could be tasted. ²³With my hands outstretched clutching the roots, I tumbled over the edge of the wall, landing face skyward on the sand cushions below, between two ridges of jutting rock. ²⁴The watchman and the two priests looked down at me; the watchman looked in horror, but the priests looked in amazement, as though I were a fallen angel whose mission had been to save their lives.

²⁵I do not know how long I lay there with my body utterly shocked. I woke in the night parched and dehydrated, confused and unable to move. ²⁶I glanced about me, frightened, trembling at the glowing green eyes of night creatures darting about me. ²⁷I sobbed for Jeremiah to revive me. I prayed for You not to let me die here, outside of the wall, for the jackals and Babylonians to prey upon. ²⁸I drew the root closer to my mouth.

²⁹Thus wrote Anatiya, to the guard of the walls of Jerusalem:

The hour before morning
you rescued me who had fallen.
³⁰You came to me and kissed me
with a mouth that burned into me like fire.
³¹Is this what you attempted with Shulamit,
when you stripped her of her mantle?
³²But my body did wake in revulsion.
My teeth did grit and my blood did boil
because of your wicked acts.
³³Before you could undo the embroidered cloth
around my waist,
a surge of life returned to me and I leapt up.
³⁴The guard was too surprised at first to react.
God will punish you according to your deeds

~WROTE ANATIYA.

³⁵I rushed into the forest and collapsed.
I realized I was still crushing the root in my palm.
I flung it away and wept over the hurt in my legs.

## 22

Thus wrote Anatiya: Jeremiah goes down to the palace of the king and the gleam of marble sets him in white fire. ²He is introducing new words into the royal lexicon; 'Justice' and 'righteousness' trill off his tongue like the exotic sounds of a foreign language. ³The stones understand the prophecy of my love. Tears trickle along their hewn channels. ⁴It will not be long before the palace is dust, before the jewel-encrusted throne is crushed under the wheels of heaven's chariots. ⁵And strangely, I feel an unusual calm. I notice Jeremiah's brow; it is not perspiring. He too, I can tell, is removed from the urgency of his message. ⁶The sway of his body is only the routine of many years prophesying. ⁷The inflections of his voice are not as much passion as they are habit, like the musicians down in coffee-alley, drumming out the same rhythm night after night, their fingers thudding the skins by rote. ⁸Jeremiah knows it is already too late. His soul packed her bags long ago. His mind is tidying up a place for his body to rest. The ruin of this palace will be his release.

⁹For thus Jeremiah speaks at the gates of the royal palace:
¹⁰With clear eyes and dry hands
and a regular pulse. ¹¹He no longer
twists in the night over doubt.
He no longer rakes his head with:
"Were I a truer prophet,
a more animated orator,
this people would not be consigned
to God-fire."

¹²You are guiltless, my love.

¹³So do not weep for the dead
and do not lament for them.
¹⁴Weep only for the unraveling of time
and the thin tangle of threads
which are our days, frayed edges
at the feet of the Weaver.

¹⁵There was a time when this land was uninhabited. ¹⁶Yellow insects hovered close to the ground, nectar glistening on their bellies. Migrating flocks alighted upon its bristling slopes, ¹⁷and sang to God new songs. ¹⁸The sand was not a scorching sudden death, but endlessly patient. ¹⁹We shall never see the land this way. Our soft footprints have left scars.

²⁰Our footprints have left impressions
in the soft flesh of this land.
²¹If Aaron or his sons were to examine it,
they would see that the impressions are deeper
than the skin of this body.
²²The hair therein has turned white.

They would declare it unclean
with a leprous infection
and send it away.
<sup>23</sup>But I wonder,
is it so lonely outside the camp?
Is it so wretched?
<sup>24</sup>To be outside the magic circle
standing in the pouring rain,
drenched and cool
and quenched.
I venture a thought:

~WROTE ANATIYA

<sup>25</sup>I think I should like it there.
Far be it from me to welcome exile,
but I daresay:
I grow faint in the heat of this camp.

<sup>26</sup>Assuredly, thus wrote Anatiya as she rocked to the steady rhythm
of Jeremiah's message to the courtiers and subjects of the king:

<sup>27</sup>I clasp my knees
and let the sun wash through me.
Curled up on the step;
<sup>28</sup>I am an unborn babe in a vessel of light.
I listen easily to the dreadful words,
and their meanings roll away in rainbows.
I can hear just beneath them,

<sup>29</sup>I can hear in your long and easy breaths
that you are relaxed.
<sup>30</sup>You are learning to let God use you.
Your mouth channels His Voice
<sup>31</sup>but your soul is curled up with me, my love.
I feel you here.

[32]I smooth my hair for you.
It is still soft as a child's,
[33]but there are lines around my eyes
and my skin is brown,
sun-spotted,
legs less limber,
a grown woman curled up like an unborn babe.
[34]We have been together this way for so long:
me on the step, small,
you, on the uppermost tier,
seven heavens high.
[35]Me the astronomer,
and you the sky.
[36]We are a pair of aging lovers
surveying the generations
with loving detachment.
[37]I realize just now
in a revelation of the heart
that you, dear love, are as silent as I.
[38]We are one and the same.
The noise around you,
the condemnations on your tongue,
are not yours.
[39]You and I are a silent stone
smoothed over by ceaseless tides.
[40]I recognize you, Jeremiah,
shy and dark.
I listen to your long, sweet breaths.
[41]Perhaps I am even
happy

[42]As I live ~ wrote Anatiya ~ if you were a signet ring upon my right
hand, I would press you into the wax and seal each of my scrolls with
your sign. [43]I would press you into the heels of my feet that every step I
left would bear your mark, indicate that you had touched me. [44]Have you

touched me? Some mornings I wake with the distinct feeling, just shy of a surety, that you have touched me in the night, spirited to my side on tiptoe and laid your hand along my neck, my arm, my belly. ⁴⁵I wake with that part of me raw and alarmed. Though I find no rash, it burns.

> ⁴⁶A wretched broken pot
> will this palace become
> and the people will stream out like a stew,
> seeping into the rubble,
> lapped up by wild dogs.
> ⁴⁷O land, land, land,
> hear my lament for you!
> The people shall be scoured . . .
> I weep not. But for you!
> ⁴⁸Your sparse greenery is so brave and so lovely.
> Would that Heaven spare your fruit and fern!
> ⁴⁹Would that angels take hold of your roots
> and blink their tears into your lacy tendrils!

## 23

Ah, the hair of Solomon's bride cascades down her shoulders as a flock of ewe-lambs down the hills of Gilead. ²Solomon's hands are two shepherds gathering up the soft woolen loops. ³Would that we could gather a nest of it; puff out a burrow with those soft tresses and nestle ourselves in . . . two mice from the cold. ⁴The Lord declares through your lips, "I Myself will gather the remnant of My flock, and I will bring them back to their pasture." ⁵I shout back teasingly, "Go ahead! If You want it done right then do it Yourself! Leave us out of it!" ⁶My eye catches a mouse scurrying under a pile, and in my mind's eye I follow it through a maze of underground tunnels. ⁷Even there you cannot hide, little one. Even as you ball yourself up, tuck up your nose and your tail to a roll of warm dust, He sees you. ⁸And none shall be missing on the day of His reckoning. ~wrote Anatiya.

⁹See the gnarled olive tree ~wrote Anatiya~ hollowed out by lightning and by rot. ¹⁰Even so, and without much effort, it raises up a true branch feathered with long green leaves that ruffle silvery in the wind. ¹¹It

manages to nourish, with its body utterly cored, a dangling of olive-fruit, rich as the coins dangling over a wealthy bride's forehead.

[12]Even so, and without much effort ~wrote Anatiya~ a green shoot will push through the devastation of Judah. Its roots will be longer than any flowering thing. [13]They will reach down and wrap around the very bones of David. They will weave through his ribs as a basket. [14]It will rise up, a righteous palm, its fronds as open fingers, and wave in the exiles, the holy remnant. [15]The soul of Deborah will meditate at the base of it. [16]All of Israel will be gathered. All of Judah will rejoice. [17]And the same timbrels that they danced with when they crossed the Sea of Reeds shall be taken up again, streaming with ribbons, when God remembers His love, and delivers us from the northlands with an outstretched hand.

[18]Concerning my prophet.

My heart is crushed within me,
all my bones are trembling
when I see, all at once,
how God intoxicates you with venomous sayings
and you stagger as one overcome by wine.
[19]A wife remembers to forget
a measure of flour or water
so she might feign flightiness to her husband,
absentmindedness to her children,
and dash back to the market
where lovers await behind sacks of grain.
[20]The husband gives signal that he is alone,
and the neighbor's wife meets him in his upper chamber
while his daughter, seeing that no one is minding,
is lured to the neighbor
who knows not that her blood is his own

~WROTE ANATIYA.

[21] Assuredly,
God presents their lewdness to you
in wads of thick tar.
[22] He paints their wickedness behind your eyelids
so you are forced to witness
their twisted bodies and lifted skirts
and hair matted with heat

~WROTE ANATIYA.


[23] But remember, my prophet,
when He shows you these repulsive things,
though they horrify and fill you with dismay
and bring a vile taste to the back of your teeth,
a rising in your throat,
[24] remember they are searching, too,
down dark and slippery pathways.
They are searching, too,
to relieve this sense of doom.
[25] Poor creations,
mistaking ecstasy for worthiness.
[26] Their deeds are ugly, Jeremiah,
but their souls are tormented beauty,
as is yours, companion of the Most High.
[27] Be careful not to coddle God with acquiescence,
but question and shiver at His condemnations.
[28] Remember the test of Abraham
concerning Sodom and Gomorrah.

[29] Assuredly, thus wrote Anatiya concerning the prophets of Jerusalem:

Comedy!
The prophets of Jerusalem
with their tubby bellies full of sweet bread,
lips dripping wine, promising good cheer.
[30] To them God's Voice is a rumble in their gut.

They have never heard it so they are never afraid.
³¹They are jesters and entertainers.
They love to see the faces smiling at them.
³²They delude the people, saying,
"All shall be well,"
and the men jab one another,
"I told you so," and feel jovial.
³³I do not smile at them.
I stand in front of the merry throng
with my hands over my ears
and my head shaking,
my posture bent with woe
and my eyes fixed on them in livid disbelief,
³⁴as if watching a man
set himself on fire.
³⁵They try not to look at me,
those lazy opportunists.
³⁶But I know that of all the people
that they coddled and catered
with their words,
it will be my face that will appear to them
in the moment of their shame.
³⁷They shall clearly perceive it.

³⁸But you, God sent,
though you did not rush in.
³⁹While you were yet in your mother's womb,
a tiny drop turning this way and that,
⁴⁰God selected a soul from the treasury of souls
for you. ⁴¹God opened the banks
and all the souls rose in reverence and
in yearning for birth.
⁴²And one soul cowered behind the gate,
terror-struck by His glory
and by a secret premonition

that this birth would be weighted
with anchors and sorrows. ⁴³And this soul,
she hid, though her dancing light deceived her,
and her muffled weeping,
which sounded like the wings of a Seraph,
gave her away. ⁴⁴She hid,
but in her fear,
her clearness spilt away from her,
limpid and shining.
⁴⁵And God said, "This is the soul of Jeremiah."
I know.

I was there, too

~WROTE ANATIYA.

⁴⁶No one knows God's closeness more than you.
No one more appreciates
God far away

~WROTE ANATIYA.

⁴⁷For God fills heaven and earth and you

~WROTE ANATIYA.

# 24

The Lord showed you two baskets of figs, one containing very good figs
and the other containing very bad figs whose innards leaked through the
weave of the basket. ²God instructs you concerning the figs, that the bad
figs represent the remnant in Jerusalem whom He will exterminate with
disgrace among the nations, and the good figs are the exiles who will return to God with all their heart and be His cherished people. ³I watch you,
patient student of God, as you absorb meaning upon meaning.

⁴But this morning, even with the dazzling God-flecks clinging
around you, I cannot take my eyes off the good figs. ⁵My body has become

an upside-down ziggurat. My ribs step inward to the point of my waist. [6]My eyes are ringed with dark hunger circles.

[7]When the word of the Lord came to you:

[8]Commandments funneled into your mouth and ignited you inside like a lantern. [9]The light of your heart blazed through your skin like the lovely silhouette of a bare woman behind the thin walls of her tent. [10]I hated the taste of my tongue at that moment, in light of your radiance. My hunger considered consuming my life. [11]The sun blazed through your fingers. I, brittle, parched, was bent at your feet. [12]I collapsed at the entrance of the Lord's House where Jeremiah was, my hands on the threshold. [13]The marble floor was a pan beneath me, heat rising into my cheek. [14]Now I, too, will be a blaze of fire, like the divine being who walked in the furnace. [15]Now I, too, will be a blaze of fire like you, my love, and we can merge as the flame of two wicks. I disintegrate in this heat, in this hunger, a withered, empty skin. [16]O my heart . . .

[17]Then a silence. God lifts suddenly as a storm does, leaving us calm with a just a rustle of damage. [18]Something soft presses against my mouth and I open my lips. [19]It is a fig, a very good fig, a first-ripened fig. [20]My eyes are soldered shut, sealed with a line of sun-blaze as with mortar. [21]I devour the fig. Immediately another is pushed into my mouth. And another and another. [22]The sweet honey covers my face and I rejoice and I laugh. I lose count of the number of figs I am fed. [23]My life is restored, moving out from my belly to my fingers and toes. The marble cools. I rise up slowly and the feeding stops. [24]The sun releases my eyes from their blindness and I look for my savior. [25]I see, not near and not far, Jeremiah, walking away with an empty basket under his arm.

[26]I weep with abandon, and the Temple walls swell with my love and amazement. [27]How little I understand You! How greatly I fear You! [28]And then suddenly You rush in and astonish me with kindness!

## 25

I walked in a daze to the center square of the city. [2]All of the inhabitants of Jerusalem were there in living ripples around my prophet. They leaned inward to listen. [3]They had played truancy for over two decades to Jeremiah's prophesies, but now that they have seen King Jeconiah and their officials, craftsmen and smiths exiled at the hands of King Nebuchadrezzar to Babylon, they have come to inquire of their fate. ⁴Thus spoke my love:

"From the thirteenth year of King Josiah son of Amon of Judah, to this day, these twenty-three years, the word of the Lord has come to me ..." ⁵Each word his lips delivered was a soft, ripe fig pressed to my mouth, its silky membrane breaking against my teeth, and the burst of sweet pulp on my tongue. ⁶He fed me with his own hands. I looked about at all the people gathered to hear my prophet. ⁷None of them knew that he had fed me with his own hands.

⁸And although they were words of slaughter he spoke, and although the people writhed and moaned at their sounding, I stood in the midst of the grimy inhabitants, head held high as if it bore a wreath of fresh lilies. ⁹I stood in the midst of those fallen countenances with my visage beaming. I was, at that instance, a bride in a sun-washed linen gown. ¹⁰Although the lumps of their bodies stood in a mass, backs to me, eyes transfixed on the bearer of terror, I am sure I saw their souls turn and gasp at my beauty. ¹¹I am sure I saw their souls part a neat aisle in their midst, and bow at the waist toward my presence. ¹²I am sure I saw two cherubs draw their wings together over Jeremiah in a wedding canopy. And although my feet remained rooted, I am sure my soul sailed steadily down that aisle, and his arms opened to me, and his mouth smiled, diamond-teeth flashing. ¹³And although he was speaking a ruinous message to them, I am sure he was uttering, "Behold, I betroth you to me forever," to me. ¹⁴And although the clanking of the sword-sharpeners could be heard from the north, I am sure there sprung a chorus of heavenly hosts chiming mirth and gladness, over the union of this silver bridegroom, over this golden bride.

¹⁵Angels descend to me from seventy worlds, bearing gifts of blessings. To them my voice is loud as cymbals. ¹⁶I cry to them, "Go to the nations that serve Babylon! Go to the land of the Chaldeans! ¹⁷Invite them as celebrants to a wedding feast of one hundred and eighty lifetimes. ¹⁸Alert them to wear their finest shade of spirit-blue. Let the worlds of the living and dead dance and rejoice at my wedding! ¹⁹And when they ask you when and at what time to arrive, ²⁰instruct them so: When the wheels of revenge are stilled. When God surrenders the settling of scores. When the cup of wrath is drained and rinsed and refilled with rain-shower. At the dawning of the world to come."

²¹For thus writes Anatiya~ Should I care about which great king enslaves which great king? I only see one man fettering his brother. ²²Should

I care whether the border of this territory is here or four cubits to the east? I only see nature's wild, jagged beauty.

²³Bring anyone to a wedding with a crescent of drummers kneeling, and he will know to tap his thigh and move his feet in dance. ²⁴Bring anyone sticks, leaves, and a kettle filled with water, and he will know to boil tea. ²⁵So a man traces his ancestry in the sand, impressively back to Japheth or Shem or Ham, so a line here, so a line there, are we not all by-products of the Potter's first creation? ²⁶Who would not scrunch his nose at the smell of sour milk? Who would not love a new dress? Who would not cry if spat upon? ²⁷Who would not dip a toe in a spring, pass a hand under a waterfall? ²⁸Who would not marvel at the moving of the stars, at the great stripe of milky white swathed across the dark? ²⁹Who would not cower before the sword? Who has not lain still in the morning, exerting a moment's drowsy contemplation, trying to remember a dream?

³⁰The world landscape is punctured with obnoxious flags. ³¹Why is one group called Tyre, Gaza, or Ashkelon? Why is the other called Ashdod, Dedan, or Buz? ³²What makes this nation Teman, Zimri, or Arabia, and yonder the land of Egypt, Moab, or Uz? ³³Is the blood of Edom, Philistine, or Ekron any weaker shade than that of Ammon, Sidon, Media, or Sheshach? ³⁴Rather, let my left hand take my right hand captive than witness one nation enslave and demolish another. ³⁵Rather, let my heart drag my feet away in chains than witness one ruler flex at the expense of another. ³⁶Let the flags of the nations be white and blank, and lifted, in the great surrender of humanity, to the day on which God's Name will be One.

³⁷Are there really any 'ends of the earth?'
Is there really any 'edge of the wilderness?'
³⁸I see the first exiles in ropes and chains
There among them is the potter.
He recognizes me and smiles.
³⁹The ropes on his arms are just garlands to him.
They do not bruise the space inside the vessel.
⁴⁰They are being led away:
the craftsmen, officials, and smiths,
walking away and away,
⁴¹but perhaps the earth is round
and there are no ends or edges,
and they are walking toward, toward . . .

~WROTE ANATIYA.

⁴²There is a gurgling beneath the sands,
the terrible sound of a man slain in the chest.
⁴³A river of blood is mounting from this
terrible wound to Jerusalem.
⁴⁴There is a rainbow above us,
but it is upside-down,
drawn taut toward earth.
God has forgotten His promise.

⁴⁵The setting sun is a slash of fresh red across the sky. God's mighty
chargers are racing forth on rays. ⁴⁶Godspeed night. Rush the darkness.
⁴⁷The twilight shadows are tormenting my eyes. ⁴⁸They are congregating
into heaps of death all over the land.

⁴⁹"Howl, you shepherds, and yell,"
cries Jeremiah. ⁵⁰The last licks
of sun set fire to a thousand foxtails,
set them loose to ignite villages
and grazing-grounds. ⁵¹The round, sweet
bleating of sheep becomes an unanimal-like
high-pitched screech with the stench of burning wool.
⁵²There is outcry from the shepherds
in their blazing tents.
⁵³"For the Lord is ravaging their pasture.
The peaceful meadows shall be wiped out
by the fierce wrath of the Lord."
⁵⁴Jeremiah's words paint images on my mind
the way an artisan decorates a vase.
⁵⁵The air over Judea is boiling
and the skirts of the city are singed.
⁵⁶Walls of fire begin to cave in
when night finally closes
and extinguishes the holocaust.
⁵⁷All that is left is the
smoke of the moon.

## 26

Thus wrote Anatiya: God is in dialogue with Himself, and little Jeremiah is the message carrier. ²At one moment the message proclaims: I will do this vengeful thing! At the next, the message amends: I will reconsider the matter. ³Meanwhile we wait under a dangling sword. Turn back! Turn back! Turn this way and that! ⁴It is an absurd dance to me. It is the eerie rocking of mourners as they warble to and fro down the streets.

⁵Thus wrote Anatiya ~ Do not make this House like Shiloh, O Lord! Where the old men are overturned with broken necks, where new mothers name their sons Ichabod, saying "The glory of God has departed." ⁶Why bother uprooting and replanting us if You are only going to uproot us and replant us again in the same place? ⁷Rather, tend us with tenderness. Garden us gently, and understand it is hard for roots to cling in arid soil.

⁸A bevy of prophets and priests ingest your sayings and it does not settle well. ⁹They grow infuriated. I watch the heat rising in their necks as you speak. ¹⁰They tense like the haunches of a cat intending to spring on prey. ¹¹All at once, God hesitates, but for a moment to inhale before flooding you again, and in that moment the predator pounces. ¹²On the very steps of the House of the Lord, even before the open archway to the glowing altar of sacrifice, they cry out, "You shall die!" ¹³They tug on your flesh, their voices and fists raised in fury. Amidst the mob I catch flashes of your face, lowered from the blows and the press of them upon you. ¹⁴A black cloud is settled upon your brow.

¹⁵I threw myself upon their backs and they instantly shoved me away, as though I contained the impurity of a corpse. ¹⁶I could not break through to you. I scratched and ripped at their skin but they would not let me through to their prisoner. ¹⁷And so I did the only thing I could think of in my madness and my fear for you. ¹⁸I flew to the altar, past the guards who were turned toward the scene, and I took hold of the silver fire pan. ¹⁹I had intended to swing it against the priests, clang it against their heads like the walls of a bell. ²⁰But when the instrument was in my hand, I was overcome with a fury, the likes of which I have never known.

²¹As they pressed into you and guffawed for your death, I raced up the altar ramp. ²²It entered my mind even as I ran up the altar ramp that no woman before me had ever been in this place. ²³That no woman's slender fingers had ever taken hold of this silver shovel. ²⁴No woman's

light step had ever scuffed against this stone in the past. And no woman would ever ascend here after me. ²⁵It struck me, even as I was rushing up the ascent, that this was profoundly sad. ²⁶That I was, at that moment something unique under the sun. ²⁷But this revelation did not abate my fury, only fed into it more. ²⁸How dare You! My fury was a cauldron of fire in my head. ²⁹And my anger at the priests was only a small flicker in the midst of the rage that overwhelmed me.

³⁰At the summit of the altar I threw my arms up, the shovel up over my head, and I slammed it down into the sacred fire. ³¹I slammed the shovel into the flames to extinguish them. To put an end to this burning. ³²Smoke collected in my eyes, lifted the tresses of my hair. ³³I could not put it out, I could not diminish the fire. ³⁴I began to scatter the flames all about, tossing shovelfuls of flame over the sides of the altar. The flames died within moments of leaving the altar. ³⁵Visions arose out of my madness: Moses, Nadav and Abihu, and Lot's wife; all those who had ever borne witness to fire raining from the sky. ³⁶And I kept shoveling. I was twirling with shovelfuls of flame and ash and scattering them in wide circles about the altar. Circles of fire. ³⁷A guard turned to me and I saw him see me before he could shout. ³⁸I leapt off the northern side of the altar, leaping over the rings that were used to fasten the heads of animals to the ground. ³⁹Romantic words entered my mind on a misplaced ribbon of thought: "Hurry, my beloved, swift as a gazelle, to the hills of spices!" ⁴⁰While you were defending yourself before the people and officials, I was ducked down and hiding in the chamber of the lambs.

⁴¹I am so practiced a stalker because of my love for you, I found my way out of the House undetected. ⁴²I found you as the officials and all the people were saying to the priests and prophets, "This man does not deserve the death penalty, for he spoke to us in the name of the Lord our God." ⁴³But you were so deeply bruised that no statement could cheer you. ⁴⁴You know too well that the people who defended you this day will abuse you in the morrow.

⁴⁵They care nothing about you. They only want to use your life to bribe Your God, ⁴⁶hoping the Lord will renounce their punishment the way He did in the days of Micah the Morashtite, all on behalf of your imploring. ⁴⁷But you are wearied of imploring. You recall that prophet's words:

⁴⁸"Her rulers judge for gifts,
her priests give rulings for a fee,
and her prophets divine for pay."

⁴⁹They want to offer your life as a gift to the Ruler who judges them.
⁵⁰God forgave iniquity in the days of Micah. God remitted transgression. Now they will think he was a truer prophet than you, for the good effect of his imploring. ⁵¹"So let Micah rise out of his grave and save them!" Jeremiah thinks, "And let me, meanwhile, keep his grave warm!"
⁵²Uriah son of Shemaiah was a young prophet at that time. His eyes and thin brow looked puzzled in disbelief at the words he was saying. ⁵³He prophesied against the city, the same as Jeremiah, but he phrased his words as suggestions rather than convictions, shy questions rather than exclamations. ⁵⁴Uriah was a watery sort of boy, greenish with eyes that drooped. ⁵⁵He often looked the way I pictured the prophet Jonah after having been spit up by the great fish. I liked Uriah, and my sympathy extended to him. ⁵⁶After Jeremiah was released, King Jehoiakim condemned this worried young prophet who always seemed seasick or God-sick, soft and waxy under the burning wick of God's presence. ⁵⁷The king's men pursued the sweet boy to Egypt and brought him to the king. ⁵⁸They slay him and threw his body, light and limp like a shred of cloth, into the burial place of the common people. ⁵⁹I visit the grave sometimes, and listen to a murmuring of souls.

## 27

It was not long after that I saw the pallor of my prophet's face shift from its celestial sheen to that of a dead man, when this word came to Jeremiah:

²Make for yourself thongs and bars of a yoke, and put them on your
    neck.
³So Jeremiah chiseled a tree trunk, and each striking blow of the hammer drowned out the sound of his sobs and gasps. ⁴I tore at my hair as I watched. I pressed my forehead to the ground while my entire body trembled in sorrow. ⁵An old locksmith fashioned a lock and closed that yoke around Jeremiah's neck, his white ivory tower neck holding his head unnaturally

erect. ⁶The words of the psalmist arose in me: "Deliver me, O God, for the waters have reached my neck; I am sinking into the slimy deep."

⁷He has always delivered God's prophecies this way, and really, this is how You have always had him, harnessed at the neck, plowing Your city. ⁸But now he is utterly humiliated, like a criminal or a beast of the field. ⁹For You, it is all metaphor, but for me, it is cruelty seeing him teeter under the weight. He was just starting to grow accustomed to the burden of You. ¹⁰He was just starting to spill your declarations with an air of nonchalance. ¹¹A tentative freedom. A withdrawal into a quiet corner of his soul. ¹²And now You have made him the baker who came to Joseph with a dream. ¹³You have lifted his head from his body and let the birds pick his flesh. He is choking! ¹⁴A flow of tears masks his entire face in a shine. There is a tremor in his voice as if the words coming from his mouth are serpents that might turn around and bite him. ¹⁵At night, he cannot lay his weary head down, so he sleeps sitting upright, nodding with the weight of the yoke. ¹⁶His hair turns white and it rolls down his back like melting snow, reflecting the sun in crystalline glints. ¹⁷His beard comes down like icicles. ¹⁸O Jeremiah, sweet boy whom I have loved since we were children, if I could spirit that yoke away, if I could heal what ails you, if I could whisk you far from Judgment and close to Mercy, I would do anything Jeremiah, ¹⁹but God guards you so tightly, and clasps His hands around your neck the way a fire clasps brightness, and I cannot (can I?) approach. ²⁰If it is any comfort, my love, I treasure you.

²¹There is an angry rash from the heat and friction of the yoke on his neck, eating into him, and at night Jeremiah writhes from the sore. And it grows worse.

²²It is amazing that a person can long for something her entire life, and the very power of that longing can make her afraid, frozen in fear. ²³And then, all at once, that fear is overcome, without any strenuous effort, by a compassion that comes with maturity. ²⁴It was not need. It was not longing. It was a sudden instinct to nurture that allowed me at once to close, in the last waking hours, the distance I have preserved so vigilantly. ²⁵Without thought, without any moment's consideration at all, I halved a melon and filled it with oil, and I walked to him as he sat under the weight of the yoke. ²⁶I walked with a sure step, in front of his sight, in front of the last reaches of sun, instinctually and unafraid. ²⁷He looked up at me through the thick bars of his eyelashes, and I did not meet his eyes, but looked away, and smiled. ²⁸I

walked behind him, without a thought or a fear in my being, as if guided, as if brought near to him, *by him*. [29]I dipped my fingers into the oil. I dipped my fingers into the oil and I rubbed it into his neck, and my slender hand slipped under the wooden yoke and I rubbed, so gently, the oil into the skin of his neck, into the rash. [30]And for those moments, God made no sound. [31]Spoke no word to him. Not a peep. [32]All the while, Jeremiah wept noiselessly, tears running down his cheeks and into his beard of icicles, rocking gently. [33]I pulled off some of the splintering wood that was irritating him. [34]I gathered his beautiful hair into my hands and smoothed it down with oil, with long soft strokes over his warm head. [35]His breathing evened and deepened. He began to fall asleep.

[36]It was only when I left him there sleeping that a star exploded inside of me and the immensity of what I had done rushed upon me. [37]I had touched him, and stroked him, and most amazingly, I had eased him into a calm slumber, with my own hands! [38]And no lightning struck me, and no God intervened, and I touched him, him, the prophet, Jeremiah, whom I love above all else. [39]How? How had I been able . . . after so many . . . after so much . . . I had touched him, simply, naturally, *instinctually* . . . these hands, my fingers. [40]I lay under a tree, some distance from Jeremiah, confused to the root of my soul, feeling that I had died suddenly, or been born anew, and I lay frozen between laughter and crying and running away and running back to him. [41]I began to violently shake and burn inside. [42]My longing became dislodged and scampered around me, a chicken without a head. [43]I felt the whole world spinning through this cosmic ocean, spinning with unimaginable rapidity. [44]I buried my face into my hands and concentrated on breathing the scent of Jeremiah's hair, a scent of apples, and oil, and melon, and high, distant breezes that rustle the tips of the Lebanon cedars.

[45]Every evening that he wore the yoke, my fear abated, and the Godstorm lifted. [46]I went to him and rubbed the oil into his neck and his hair while he wept and rocked, and his breathing softened and deepened. [47]I returned to my sleeping place dizzy, my soul awash in the purest joy. I blessed. I blessed being, and the Supreme Being. I was swept up in confusion, in the spin of the earth.

[48]One evening as I touched him, I saw the men of King Nebuchadnezzar's army marching, bearing the holy vessels out of the House of the Lord. I recognized the silver shovel slung over the back of a Babylonian soldier. [49]The shovel was carrying in its pan a reflection of the North Star, and it winked at me.

## 28

Hananiah son of Azzur stands in the House of the Lord, tall as Saul. ²He is alluring, with the stature and features of a prince of Egypt. ³He is an enlightened man, indeed, but no prophet. ⁴He approached Jeremiah in the presence of the priests and all the people. ⁵My sweet seemed bent and tired. ⁶The skin of his face is furrowed. Like a copper goblet, it is elegantly engraved. ⁷Only his brow remains as smooth as it was when he was a young boy. ⁸His hair flows down in cool streams, pouring into the river of his beard. ⁹I kneel attentive in the front of the people. I no longer hide in the shadows. ¹⁰My love is too beautiful to lurk. ¹¹Hananiah has a penetrating voice, deep and mesmerizing. ¹²As he speaks, he hypnotizes the people with his hands. ¹³He uses Jeremiah as God does, as a prop. ¹⁴At the moment Hananiah declares, "I hereby break the yoke of the king of Babylon," ¹⁵I thought I saw Jeremiah glance at me, or perhaps just a thought of me crossed his mind.

¹⁶Jeremiah responded with a hearty and immediate "Amen! May the Lord do so!" ¹⁷And I understood him as no one else. ¹⁸His "amen" did not intend to convey agreement. ¹⁹Rather, when he said "amen" to Hananiah, he was saying to God, "Get me out!" He was crying for help. ²⁰How long will he have cares on his mind and grief in his heart all day? ²¹He knows that Hananiah is no prophet, but O! to have the luxury of foolishness! ²²To be able to nod and "amen" false prophets and sleep soundly with glad tidings resounding in your ears! ²³His "amen" did not intend to convey belief. ²⁴Rather, when Jeremiah said "amen" to Hananiah, he was saying to God, "Look at me! Answer me, O Lord! Restore the luster to my eyes! ²⁵Free me from You, and let me fade into the wall of men, be with them, drink with them, laugh and die with them! This loneliness is unbearable." ²⁶God subsequently filled Jeremiah's mouth with words of challenge to Hananiah, but I know the "amen" was his own.

²⁷Hananiah removed the yoke from Jeremiah's neck and broke it in the presence of all the people. ²⁸They cheered uproariously at Hananiah's performance, and Jeremiah relaxed his head, his hand on the back of his neck, and he gasped and wept at his release. ²⁹But I was filled with a selfish pain. ³⁰I knew at once that his aura had regained its unseen metal shield. ³¹That I would once again be paralyzed from approaching him and touching him. ³²When the yoke was removed, I was removed as well. ³³Perhaps I was God's recompense to Jeremiah when he was in

his deepest misery and humiliation. [34]Perhaps I was only able to draw near to him when his perfection was marred in some way, by a rash on the skin of his neck. [35]He was suddenly as distant to me as a solitary star, nestled into an enveloping night.

[36]Jeremiah returned to Hananiah and said, "You broke bars of wood, but you shall make bars of iron instead. This year you shall die, for you have urged disloyalty to the Lord." [37]Hananiah blanched and turned away from the people. [38]He gathered himself together and bowed graciously to Jeremiah, threw his hands out valiantly to the people in blessing, and departed from the House of the Lord. [39]As bars of iron rust, Hananiah's long body became rough and flaky as with rust. [40]His hair fell out. His strength shrank inward, and in the seventh month he died. [41]Jeremiah went to his open graveside. He stared into the grave with his body leaning inward, almost teetering. [42]He was wistful and far away, inquiring of Hananiah's soul about death, about afterlife. [43]He scooped down his body and began to fill the grave with his hands. [44]I longed to help him, and I willed my body with all of my might to go to the mound, but my passion had me stunned. [45]My hands felt not like the slender fingers that smoothed under his yoke, but rather like the mauling paws of some fur-coated beast. [46]All I could do was turn and run away over the hills, and wash my burning face in the river.

# 29

I lay upon a dune. My limbs stretch out from me like lizards, barely visible in the sand. [2]Before me, I watch as King Jeconiah, the queen mother, the eunuchs and officials of Judah and Jerusalem are marched into exile. [3]They appear to me as Hebrew text marching across a roll of parchment. [4]Their ink silhouettes contort into letters on the landscape and the sun sears through them in frames of white fire. I read the line of exiles as they tip over the horizon.

[5]I am frail as a glass figurine poised on a ledge. [6]You are filled with beaming, with the distant star-rays of Heaven's first light. [7]Your face is a pool of cool, clear water into which the spirit of Moses peers. [8]His face is unveiled and emanating an ethereal shine, an even richer glow than the one from which the wandering Israelites shielded their eyes, and you are his reflection, rippled by passing days. [9]Your colors drain down the icicles

of your long beard and spill into rainbows in your footprints. ¹⁰You are carrying a roll of parchment under your arm.

¹¹You sit and pen a letter to send to the elders of the exile community. You shall not forget them. ¹²You pen a letter to our priests and prophets in a foreign land. ¹³Your body becomes limp and your head bows in fatigue, slowly, ever lower, until your face is pressed against the parchment, your hair spread over the letter in silver rays, and you sleep. ¹⁴Your body was once sturdy as a post, with the royal stride of a chosen prince. ¹⁵I once imagined that if you should miss a step, you would stumble and slip into the air, caught on a wing of soft wind. ¹⁶You were as light, and unearthly. But constant exposure to immeasurable sorrow has weathered and weakened you. ¹⁷Old sorrows have congealed into pockets of your flesh and have added weight to your body and breath. ¹⁸Now you are less like the swaying palm, and more like the wide, red, rocky pillars of Timna. How I love you, deeper still.

¹⁹I creep over to you, delighting in the soft whistle in your heavy, slumbered breath. ²⁰It sounds like the coo of a bird hidden in your breast. ²¹I peer between the rivulets of your hair and read the first lines of your letter: "Build houses in Babylon and live in them, plant gardens and eat their fruit. ²²Take wives and beget sons and daughters; and take wives for your sons, and give your daughters to husbands, that they may bear sons and daughters. ²³Multiply there, do not decrease."

²⁴I burst suddenly into tears. They well up from the deepest part of me. ²⁵These are the same tears stunted after my father abandoned us. ²⁶The same tears swallowed at the death of my mother. Tears of my aging. ²⁷Tears that I would never fulfill Jeremiah's simple command: I would never have children, never give my daughters to husbands, never rejoice in my sons taking wives. ²⁸He and I will decrease! ²⁹When we die, there will be less love and less longing and fewer great looping spirals of scrolls packed with poetry, and less promise, and less meaning, and less God-sensitive listening, and fewer prophecies, and less spirit and fewer words that come crashing through firmaments, and less passion. ³⁰Even the blast of the shofar will be less resounding. ³¹I look at the sleep of this prophet, this man-who-will-decrease, and it is not a sleep of fatigue. ³²It is a sleep of utter misery, of a sorrow that one could not bear in the waking hour. ³³The sweat along his hairline, the wheezing, the breathing which is like gasping. ³⁴I want to touch him, but without the yoke he is untouchable.

³⁵I know that this is a letter to all of the exiles in Babylon, but I know deeper. ³⁶I know in truth, my love, that you are writing this letter to me. ³⁷To me, this is no command. It is a commiseration. ³⁸Does it bring you any comfort that there is another who shares this fate, another who has chosen to decrease, if only to love you? ³⁹Or does it trouble you more, guilt you that I have been swept up in the whirlwind, with no gardens and no offspring? ⁴⁰O Jeremiah! Even more than my sadness over the house we will never build and the children we will never have, I weep over the little phrase that spilt from your quill, "Plant gardens and eat their fruit." ⁴¹I see you, in my mind's eye, kneeling in a soft, foreign soil, raking your delicate hands through the brown earth, which is moist and sweet-smelling, in the dappled light of a lush overhang, ⁴²where dewy-sweet apple blossoms are splayed like stars in a deep green sky, and pomegranates burst at the downiest touch, casting sugared rubies into shorn emerald grasses. ⁴³That garden is as far from you as this promised land was from Moses,~ wrote Anatiya.

⁴⁴You stir and your eyes flutter. I back into the shadows. Enfolded here, I am suddenly comforted. ⁴⁵I realize: when God created man and woman, He commanded them saying, "Be fruitful and multiply." ⁴⁶When Jeremiah wrote a letter to the exiles of Babylon, he commanded them saying only, "Multiply." ⁴⁷He does not say to be fruitful. For who can be fruitful in a foreign land? Who can sing songs on alien soil? ⁴⁸There on the poplars, they will hang up their lyres. ⁴⁹They will multiply and plant and increase, but without music. ⁵⁰While here in this land, you and I will decrease. ⁵¹But we will take it upon ourselves to fulfill the first half of God's original twofold command. We will be fruitful. ⁵²We will measure our words like cups of flour with which, someday, people will knead and bake and sop up what remains of life, and live. ⁵³Our fruitfulness will sustain the world.

⁵⁴The exiled prophets and priests in Babylon read the letter from Jeremiah with tremendous amusement. ⁵⁵They ridiculed the words, "Plant gardens and enjoy their fruit." ⁵⁶They laughed heartily with jiggling belly-rolls and said, "That boy has finally gone mad!" ⁵⁷They wander in a foreign land, through a city's strange maze of zigzag walkways, sniffing the strange scent of burnt honey in the air, and sour milk, fingers dragging along ridged stone, all textures not their own. ⁵⁸The air is surely prickled with unfamiliarity. ⁵⁹They trail behind the self-proclaimed prophet Shemaiah, no coin in their pocket. They joust and adore him. ⁶⁰He walks proudly, unaware of the curse that is being laid upon him and his offspring.

## 30

The word comes to you saying: Write a scroll. ²Your long elegant fingers gather around the quill. ³God dictates His message in your ear in low tones; like an illiterate pauper, He begs your service. ⁴(I have seen those men and women employing, for mere morsels, a scribe in the market. The scribe records their messages in letters to their families in the hills. ⁵In every inscription the scribe hides his name in the upper right corner. Baruch. I watch him sometimes. I read the hearts of the people over his shoulder. ⁶There is something lovely about him.)

⁷Thus writes Anatiya:

I seek relief.
I long to wean myself from you.
I wander about the city,
⁸and with each outing I stay away longer,
though with each turn you appear in a haunting.
⁹There is terror all around.
The people are starving,
and there are soldiers leering,
but I am skilled at being in the shadows.
¹⁰So this is the instrument of Your wrath, O God?
There are orphans cowering in every dark place;
¹¹Jacob's favorite son in the dark of the pit.

¹²One day ~ writes Anatiya ~ one little girl, black-ringed eyes, beautiful, an emerald shoot, frightened . . . I let her crawl into my lap and I kiss her on her brow and all over her face. ¹³She does not cry, but lavishes in my attention. We cling to each other until the heavy isolation withdraws.

¹⁴She curls in my breast
and while she sleeps I ward off the night visions

~ WRITES ANATIYA.

[15]The girl follows close behind me
and scavenges nuts and grains to appease me.
[16]Through the girl, others soon discover
the refuge of my calm
and the delivery of my quiet.
[17]Soon the shadows I inhabited so long
are teeming with orphans

~ WRITES ANATIYA.


[18]They seek my arms to hold them.
They seek my lap in which to lay their fatigue.
[19]I speak into the soft skin of their necks,
telling them, "Have no fear."
They understand the movement of my lips.

[20]I become the holder of children,
mother of the shadow-dwellers.
[21]Let God go on avenging.
I will hug.
[22]Let God twist the knife so the injury is incurable.
I will still hug and embrace and kiss.
[23]Is there anything more holy than the tears of an orphan?
My dress is dampened in them.
My face is soaked in their weeping.
[24]Their tears penetrate my pores
and the lines on my face disappear.
[25]The signs of my aging vanish
as I absorb each drop
from their wide moon-eyes.

[26]They confide in me stories of being forgotten,
confident I will not also forget.
[27]Eventually, there are a hundred children who gather,
and the night stretches out long enough for me to hold each one.

<sup>28</sup>In the day they go out in search of food,
and many do not come back.
<sup>29</sup>But they are replaced,
like the children of Job,
but it brings me no comfort

~ WRITES ANATIYA.

<sup>30</sup>One morning I journey to the hills,
to the trees who were my friends
in the days of my youth;
my lovers
in the times of my sickness over you,
those knobby fingers that broke my virgin seal.
<sup>31</sup>The moment I step into their lattice of branches
and brush my cheek to their sweet gray moss,
and watch the silver-green fringe of their leaves
flutter in cedary breezes,
a part of me I did not know was dying
is resuscitated with a great gust of God-breath.
<sup>32</sup>With leaping legs I dance,
with long arches and languid limbs
and my hair swelling up and out in soft billows
I dance as a tree whose roots are all at once
unfettered.
<sup>33</sup>When suddenly a creeping comes over me, a child out of the midst;
he comes near, that he may approach me

~ WRITES ANATIYA.

<sup>34</sup>And who would be hiding here in this grove?
And who would approach me in my sacred circle?
<sup>35</sup>And is he of the world of people, or is he of the world of God?

<sup>36</sup>For lo, his face is the face of an angel,
and his eyes are three-sides white

and their center pale as sky,
the likes of which I have never seen.
[37]His hair is a white-gold,
the color of the sun striking Jerusalem.
[38]His body is reed-thin
and swallowed in an amber light
that had no source other than his own self.

[39]In him, I recall the child Jeremiah when God's Voice first swept him
over. [40]I fall to my knees before this boy, and drop my head into my hands
and weep.

## 31

Thus spoke the child:
"Have no fear and do not weep."
[2]I raised my eyes to him and wondered in my heart,
'Who are you, celestial child?'
[3]And he spoke:
"My name is Ezekiel. I am mortal."
[4]I bolted upright, bewildered,
for he had heard and answered my unspoken thoughts.
[5]"Yes, I do see,
and I do hear.
Far beyond what is stamped in the sky."
[6]My eyes were a burst fountain and I wept over
the pent-up loneliness of my silence.
[7]The child Ezekiel came and put his arms around my shoulders.
He knelt with me upon the ground.
[8]My lips formed the words, 'I am Anatiya.'
[9]He stroked my head with his small hand
and responded, "I know, fair daughter of Zion.

I know who you are.
[10]I have studied the imprint of your spirit here in these woods."

¹¹My face flushed brightly and my tears continued in rivulets.
"No, no," Ezekiel whispered. "No shame."
¹²He swept up my tears with his fingers
and drew them along the inside of his lips.
¹³"Hush now, Anatiya, the desert trees love you.
They laugh with you.
Even now I hear them. Listen."
¹⁴I heard nothing but his heart, and with each beat
the light that clung to him rippled.
¹⁵He pressed his cheek to mine
and his hair was soft as warm water.
¹⁶He whispered as he held me,
"I know. I see it, too. And beyond.
Rest awhile, beauty.
Dream of the waking day,
O heart of a prophet."

¹⁷Ezekiel cradled my face in his hands.
He fixed his sky-eyes to mine,
"O yes, I know that too.
¹⁸You are the bride of Jeremiah's soul.
And truly, little fawn,
he knows it, too, for he is a prophet of the Lord.
¹⁹And though he cannot turn to you,
your face is before him always.
²⁰This and more is revealed to me,
for I live all at once in this time,
in a past time,
and in a future time as well.
²¹I live in three awarenesses.
I live the planting, the uprooting, and the aftergrowth.
²²I live in exodus, in exile, and in return
all at once, and so I know."
²³He laced his fingers into my own,
a child's hands, beautiful as starlight.

²⁴I kissed their smooth palms
and an immeasurable comfort settled on my heart.
'And so,' I smiled, 'Jeremiah knows my love.'

²⁵All at once I understood
the vast difference between Jeremiah and Ezekiel.
²⁶Jeremiah is filled with God's wrath,
while in this child the wrath is tempered
with a constant outpouring of Divine love
and a wash of mercy.
²⁶"It is true," Ezekiel responded.
"Jeremiah receives his visions from the left,
and I receive my visions from the right,
as well as from the mirror that shines.
²⁷I know you do not understand.
But be assured, sweet bride,
God is One, and God's love is the Same.
²⁸But when the light of that love passes
through the prism of mortality,
through the sapphire pavement,
it is refracted, and we see
what seems to be the semblance
of red and black,
blue and yellow . . .
when, in truth, all is white,
all is pure,
all is One"

~ WROTE ANATIYA.


²⁹Thus spoke the child:
"Restrain your eyes from shedding tears.
³⁰You are a little bit Rachel when you cry,
weeping for her children.
³¹But there is reward for your labor.

For you are not only the heart of the prophet,
Anatiya, Jeremiah's unwed bride,
but you are yourself a prophet of the Lord.
<sup>32</sup>And this you must remember.
Your disciples are many:
the orphans in the street,
the desert trees, nymphs, and spirits

~ WROTE ANATIYA.

<sup>33</sup>They shall teach in your name,
and there is hope for your future

~ WROTE ANATIYA.

<sup>34</sup>Even I

Even I have come to this grove to learn from you,
to study the footprints your dancing leaves in the sand."
<sup>35</sup>He touched my lips.
"For though you are no orator, you are filled with oracles.
How I envy your love."
<sup>36</sup>The child stroked my neck and lifted my hair, twisting it into braids.
"If only I had such a love as yours, Anatiya,
<sup>37</sup>Anatiya, I love you.
You will inspire many loves,
my priestess, my prophetess,
love's matriarch."
<sup>38</sup>My tears welled over and the child spun them
into circles on my cheeks.
"You will survive this apocalypse, Anatiya,
have no fear."
<sup>39</sup>I threw my arms around him fiercely.
"And for the sake of your love, this people will be restored"

~ WRITES ANATIYA.

⁴⁰The child continued:

"At this moment, my love,

your husband is lamenting.

⁴¹He is chastising Heaven on account of Ephraim.

Jeremiah sustains the world with his righteousness.

⁴²You will return to him, O Maiden Israel.

You will return to him, your love commands it.

⁴³You will run to him and fall at his feet

and court him the way a man courts a woman."

⁴⁴Thus spoke the child: "I shall make for you here a shrine. A flat stone heaped with sweet-smelling sprigs. ⁴⁵I shall write on the side of the altar:

The Lord bless you

by the merit of the righteous woman,

O holy Anatiya!"

⁴⁶I sat with my arms wrapped around my knees as I watched the child build an altar, bustling about with fresh twigs. ⁴⁷He poured fine oil over the heap and declared, "I shall call this place 'Anatot-Shelmalah,' the Upper Anatot. This is your temple, a place where sparrows make their nests." ⁴⁸He rushed to me and kissed me on the mouth. He said:

"At this moment, your husband is awaking from a deep and pleasant sleep.

⁴⁹Return to him, fair maiden, and one day soon you and I shall dance to angel-choirs in Paradise." ⁵⁰I held him to me and then I turned to rush back to the one my soul loves. ⁵¹As I turned, Ezekiel's words trailed after me: "There is a man who is watching you. He is more of earth than of sky. He will bring you face to face with the one your soul loves. This I know and more."

⁵²I run swiftly into the city squares and in an instant I have found my love. ⁵³I rush toward him and fling myself upon the ground before his feet. ⁵⁴I hear Jeremiah pause in his prophesying. I know he has glimpsed my face, smoothed by tears like a river-stone, without any lines. ⁵⁵I keep my head down at his feet, which are coated with dust. (O, to be that dust!) ⁵⁶I feel the heat of his hand reach down to touch my head, hesitate, and then withdraw. ⁵⁷He walks away, to the next square, to the next oration.

⁵⁸I laugh to God: "Go on and tug him. I don't care! You may have him by Your leash, but his heartstrings are bound up in me!"

⁵⁹I follow Jeremiah and crouch among his listeners
and I can see he is disconcerted.
And there is a blush on his cheek!

⁶⁰Thus writes Anatiya:
I have realized a power in me through my encounter with the child.
⁶¹I stir up love into roaring waves.
I cast a glisten into dull eyes.
⁶²My love is a great river that bursts its banks
and gushes from the portents of the sky,
a flood that none can hold back,
washing over towers and walls.

~ WRITES ANATIYA.

⁶³Love's matriarch! Untouched by my own lover,
my desire overwhelms and spills from me in torrents.
⁶⁴My love cannot be measured, nor can its foundations ever be
    fathomed. ⁶⁵As I contemplate the infinity of my love, a great
    miracle is mustered up out of the depths of my musings. The sky
    rains! Great ropes of rain descend, in a great, splashing rush!
⁶⁶Everyone leaps up! raising their hands to the heavens. I spin about
    and open my mouth to the cosmic fount. ⁶⁷The orphans, my friends,
    run out from the shadows with joyous songs and shouts. ⁶⁸And
    for one moment, the city is rebuilt in spirit and in essence. For one
    moment, the flung-out circles of children grasping hands become
    the indestructible bricks of a new house and a new covenant. ⁶⁹For
    one moment, Jeremiah looks at *me* in amazement. For one moment,
    all is good, and carpets of tiny flower-buds spring up beneath us.
⁷⁰For one moment we are free and healed, the heat of the sky is
    cooled, the thirst of the land is quenched, the faces of the people are
    shining, puddles lap our ankles, and love is fulfilled.
⁷¹A moment later, the sun dries the city back to its senses, and to its
    sorrow.

## 32

Miriam came to me in a night-vision. She materialized out of the desert; her black robes swirling behind her, and her hair rolling outward like snakes. ²Her face was frightening . . . her mouth drawn tight as a bow (perhaps her tongue was an arrow!), and her eyebrows were knit into a point. ³Her eyes blazed with black fire and her lashes framed them in spikes. She was dazzling, but she filled me with terror. ⁴She clutched me around my waist and transported me across the dunes. I could no longer see the fires of Jerusalem, and the stars themselves retreated. ⁵We came to a large well whose water constantly overflowed so that Miriam sloshed through the water as we approached. ⁶Then, without a word and before I could draw a breath, she thrust me into the well. I kicked and flailed my arms, but the water held me locked in its depths. ⁷When I thought I might die, she yanked me out by my hair. I awoke sputtering, and the orphans of Jerusalem comforted me. ⁸My clothes, my hair, my body were soaked, and smelled of perfume.

⁹While the army of Babylon besieged the city walls, my longing scratched at the prison cell where Jeremiah was confined. ¹⁰One day I saw a man approach with a gait similar to my love's. He asked to see the son of Hilkiah and was admitted into the prison. I wondered after him.

¹¹"He is Jeremiah's cousin, Hanamel, come to sell him land in Anatot." I turned and saw a man with a soft, familiar smile. ¹²"I am Baruch, the scribe. You shine." I blinked.

¹³"Um, I mean, I did not mean to just say it like that, but . . . you shine. You do. You simply . . . like a water creature. You glisten. I'm sorry, you just, you do." ¹⁴He laughed nervously. In my life, no one had ever spoken to me in such a friendly, easy manner. ¹⁵I remembered him, the scribe from the market place. ¹⁶"I know that you do not speak, or cannot speak. I, I know this because I have seen you, I mean I have watched you, not . . ." ¹⁷he laughed and looked down at his sandals, "not the way you watch Jeremiah, of course," ¹⁸he smiled a grand warm smile. "No one could watch the way you watch, but, I watch. I watch you. You, well I said it already, but you do. You shine."

[19]I stared at this man who seemed so casual, so relaxed, in the midst of a city gripped by war and starvation, with the weight of heaven sagging above it, brewing with fire and brimstone, and here this man found it still possible to shuffle his sandals, smile, and talk lightly. He has been watching me?

[20]"I know you love him, I mean, the way you watch with those eyes, which are so, you know, pow! wide and steady and intense. [21]So, I do not mean to make you feel in any way as if, well, I do not want anything from you, I just, well, besides that you shine, God! I look at you and I get thirsty! I mean, no, no! Not wolf-thirsty, not like I have to . . . I mean, doe-thirsty. Little doe, lapping at a stream." [22]Baruch laughed. "I am a good scribe, woman, but I do not have a way with words!"

[23]This man, he was plain. Shorter than I by almost a head, with thick brown hair and a round, full beard, a soft-looking beard, soft-looking cheeks. [24]Round eyes (doe eyes?), shaggy and comfortable with strong arms but tender hands with ink stains upon his fingers. [25]He had olive-rich skin, earthy . . . "more of earth than of sky."

[26]"It is terrible, I know, that he is in prison. But it could just be the very safest place in this city right now! If you think about it . . . I, well, we share a love for him, you know. [27]He is my friend, I would die for him. I believe him, too. I believe his words. As much as he frightens, as much as his words jab at hearts, I feel safe as his follower. [28]I, I know you feel that way too. I, woman, I love you!" [29]Baruch grabbed my two hands in his. I jumped back but I did not pull them away. I was stunned. [30]"I mean, I ache for you. I dream about you. I toss and turn over you, your curves, your hips, the gold in you, the shine. I get thirsty, I mean, my mouth gets all dry, my tongue is like a leather hide. It flops inside my mouth, a dead thing. I, I . . . my hand shakes, I drop my quill . . . your hair, I mean those long twists and turns, I just. . . ." [31]He dropped my hands and looked at the ground, but not sadly, and not in shame, for there were still dimples in his cheeks from smiling.

[32]"I just . . ." Baruch lifted his eyes to mine and shrugged. "Well, I said it. How is that? You are a beautiful woman in love with a prophet of the Lord, and I am a scribe in love with you. [33]You will never take him away from God, I will never take you away from him, and there it lies. So you and I? [34]We may as well be friends, as we share in this unique life predicament. Friends?"

<sup>35</sup>I just stood, mouth open, staring at this man. Inside I was spinning. <sup>36</sup>Friends? What does it mean to be a friend? To have a friend? <sup>37</sup>Is there any emotion between passion and disinterest? Do I have it in my heart to care for a friend, and who is this man, this scribe? <sup>38</sup>The man with Jeremiah's gait appeared again and beckoned to Baruch. He bowed slightly to me and said, "Your love is summoning me. Shall I pass on any message from you to him?"

<sup>39</sup>I felt my face blanch in fear.

<sup>40</sup>"Do not worry, woman. Your secrets are safe in here." Baruch tapped his heart and followed Hanamel into the prison compound.

<sup>41</sup>When Baruch returned he was not surprised to see me. Foolish thoughts arose in my mind: I hope he knows I am not waiting here for him! <sup>42</sup>He certainly realizes that I am here only for Jeremiah. <sup>43</sup>Of course he knows this, he watches me. He watches me? How is it that I have not noticed him before? Am I so focused on the object of my affections that I am left utterly unaware of my periphery? <sup>44</sup>And now that he has stepped out of that periphery, now that this man has risen off of the backdrop and into my life, and confessed to me, and drawn me in, how does this affect my focus, infect it, compromise my singular mission with a shrug of the shoulder, with a sweet smile, with a distraction called friendship? <sup>45</sup>Who am I if not anonymous? So different than the orphans in the street . . . this man sits in the market, in the light of the day, for all to engage. <sup>46</sup>He is from the world of the living, more of earth than of sky, whereas I have settled into the world of spirits and prophets and phantoms and dreams. Will he yank me out of my element? Expose me? <sup>47</sup>I call on the spirits of David and Jonathan: What is a friend?

<sup>48</sup>This man, he fills me with questions. This man riddles me with questions.

<sup>49</sup>"Greetings, friend," Baruch said. "Jeremiah asked me to take these documents, this deed of purchase, the sealed text and this opened one, to Anatot to be buried there in a jar so that they may last a long time. Care to come along?"

<sup>50</sup>Jeremiah asked me . . .

Jeremiah asked me . . .

Jeremiah asked me . . .

My prophet speaks to this man? He trusts him? <sup>51</sup>He places documents
into his little earthy hands?

<sup>52</sup>"Come along, woman. He is in prison anyway. I assure you you
will not miss a thing. <sup>53</sup>You can hold the documents. Cradle them like the
baby of your dreams. I will show you the land that he bought in Anatot.
<sup>54</sup>When that dawning that he prophesies about finally arrives, I am sure
he will live there, and you, his sultry spy, as well."

<sup>55</sup>I stood transfixed.

<sup>56</sup>"Unfreeze yourself, woman!" Baruch laughed and then stopped
abruptly. He took a step back and touched his beard. <sup>57</sup>"Look at you!
Shining in the sun! I," he slapped his hands onto his knees and shook
his head back and forth. "I say, I am mad for you. <sup>58</sup>Oh! If I had my in-
struments with me right now, I would sketch a portrait of you just, just
standing there, right there, but of course naked you know. To show all
of the shine of you!" <sup>59</sup>This man laughed again and then swiftly took up
my hand. He brushed his lips against it and then said in a whisper close
to my face, "If I did not know you were mute, I would think you were
speechless."

<sup>60</sup>I joined him and Hanamel on their journey to Anatot.

<sup>61</sup>Baruch ferreted me under the wall and we ducked among the cam-
els of the last merchant's caravan. <sup>62</sup>As darkness fell, Baruch and Hanamel
pitched a tent. <sup>63</sup>He lay down a burlap mat and offered it to me, saying, "It
is no cloud of down for you, beloved, but it is the best this scribe can offer."
<sup>64</sup>Hanamel built a fire and we boiled tea and warmed bread. I sat with my
knees huddled up to my nose, peaking at these two men, one, the cousin,
with traces of Jeremiah in him, the other with none at all.

<sup>65</sup>"This woman, you know, is in love with your cousin the prophet,"
Baruch said to Hanamel. <sup>66</sup>I huddled even lower behind my knees. Is this
a friend? <sup>67</sup>I must feel the same as Moses, when he realized, "the thing
is known!" and fled to Midian. How far would I need to go to flee to
Midian?

<sup>68</sup>Hanamel scarcely glanced at me. He mumbled with a full mouth,
"She looks a fine and sturdy wife."

<sup>69</sup>"She is!" He winked at me.

<sup>70</sup>"But Jeremiah has no time for a wife. That city has her legs wrapped
around him tight." Hanamel gulped his tea. "But with a city he will not sire
sons!"

[71]"It may, perhaps, be so, but Jeremiah loves this woman all the same."

[72]Jeremiah loves this woman? Me? Has my love spoken of me to this furry-faced smiling man? [73]O, love seems so much easier in illusion than in plain spoken truth. I pressed my hands around my empty cup, drawing the last of its heat into my fingers. [74]I curled up on the burlap mat and wound a lock of hair (those twists and turns) around my hand. My thoughts were all fragmented, cast about me. [75]I have been plucked out of a dream . . . jolted into the world of the living, the world of tea-around-the-fire, talking and winking and gesturing, the world of sharing-tents and laughter-over-little-things as opposed to hysterics over some revelatory absurdity. [76]And what to do in this world but wind a lock of hair? [77]This world void of metaphor, but filled instead, with myriad tiny domesticities . . . an outstretched hand, a clumsy compliment, a burlap mat, and a furry beard . . . a cloud of brown down for you, beloved . . . sleep comes.

## 33

While Jeremiah was still in the prison compound, we continued our journey to Anatot. I walked with my eyes forward, but my intention focused on the man in the corner of my eye, walking beside me. [2]My short self-proclaimed 'friend.' A man who is thirsty for me, and speaks kindly, lightly. He is chewing a carob scythe.

[3]I can smell Anatot. Can I describe the scent of home? That the scent of home can linger even when the people and the dwelling-places have long since vanished? [4]It is a mingling of moist soil and weed-pollen, sweet manure and sun-sizzled wheat. [5]The smell of my mother's hands.

[6]"The stone wall is gone
and the garden is rubbish.
[7]The roof has collapsed and the fire-hole is cold.
Though I have traveled the land top to bottom,
home still remains the one place I know,"

recited Baruch. I looked at him, surprised.

[8]He said, "My grandfather taught me that song. He claimed it was composed by the generation that crossed the desert. [9]I asked him if

the Israelites were nostalgic for Goshem, but he said it was written for Jerusalem, which never made sense to me. ¹⁰How does one have nostalgia for a place he's never been?" ¹¹He smiled tenderly at me and added, "Maybe it was written for Anatot."

¹²If I could, I would tell Baruch how easy it was to be nostalgic for a place you have never been. ¹³He interrupted my thoughts and said, "Show me the place of your youth." ¹⁴He picked up my hand and gestured that I should guide him. I stood still, looking at my hand in his.

¹⁵He laughed. "You are a golden stalk of wheat, planted in one spot, picking up the breeze. You are lovely. Lovely! But pull up your roots, woman, and pick up your legs and walk!"

¹⁶Against my will, and much to my embarrassment, I smiled. I turned away quickly and walked a bit in front of him in the desperate hope that this man would not see, but by the squeeze on my hand, I am sure that he did.

¹⁷And just to play with my shame, this man, this friend, would walk faster and faster to try to glimpse my face, and I in turn would walk faster still, until we two were running, running toward my childhood home. ¹⁸And when we at last arrived, it was too late for me. ¹⁹I pulled my hand from his and covered my face with both of my hands, and I laughed, perhaps for the first time, perhaps for the only time in my life. ²⁰I laughed and it sounded like panting. I doubled over, shaking, and tears came to my eyes. ²¹My cheeks burned with shame and embarrassment. I felt humiliated in front of this stranger, this friend, but the laughter did not stop. ²²I lowered myself to the ground because the world was spinning. ²³Baruch laughed heartily as he watched me. Full-throated and trumpet-loud.

²⁴Then he took me in his arms. He peeled my fingers from my face like a skin from a rosy fruit. ²⁵The laughter stopped. He kissed my salty eyelids and down my streaked cheeks. And he put his warm mouth over mine. ²⁶I pulled away and buried my face again, and wept.

²⁷He held me even so, and said softly, "Come, forgive me, bride of Jeremiah. If I just hold you, like this, if I just, you know, hold you. ²⁸I won't kiss your mouth, though I thirst for you. ²⁹I won't kiss your lips, woman, though it is against everything I feel and everything I want." ³⁰Baruch held me close to him and stroked my hair. "And, you know? Just now I am thinking, I just think that . . . it is not that you love him. ³¹That is not why I won't kiss you and kiss you and kiss you. For I am an ordinary man, and just as selfish and greedy, and lustful as any man. ³²No, woman. Give me

no honor because I resist. It is no favor to you, no respect for your love. [33]It is, I really believe, it is that prophet, and that God. They have ganged up on me and sealed you like a pent-up fountain. [34]When I touched your lips for a moment? Had you not pulled away so quickly I would have pulled myself away . . . [35]I was filled with a rush of fear . . . no, a certain terror that made me quake. And I know it is God and His prophet ganged up on me. [36]But they let me hold you. And they let me give you laughter. I suppose I am their gift to you, a prize. [37]But not the prize you really want, so I am a sorry gift. A jester for the queen who makes her throw her head back in laughter, but not in ecstasy. And what for me? [38]What for me?"

[39]I was filled, at once, with pity for this man, and I held him in return, and I kissed his brow lightly. [40]We wept together, until we fell asleep in the field in each other's arms.

[41]Awareness crept over me softly, seeping into my dreams. I opened my eyes and was not stunned to see Baruch's face over me, eclipsing the afternoon sun. [42]He was fanning out my hair in rays and smiling. He kissed my cheeks. [43]He said, "While the city is whoring with false gods, and the people prostituting themselves in the temples, here in my arms is a virgin, with full breasts and a woman's hips. How have you survived here?"

[44]I sat up, brushed myself off and adjusted my robes. I looked toward Jerusalem and wondered after my prophet. Baruch followed my gaze.

[45]"I will bring you your heart's desire, woman. I will take you to your love." I knew this man to be telling the truth, and there in the golden glow, and the steady buzz of insects and heat, I threw my arms around him and held him to me. [46]His arms were limp at his side, but I could hear the blood in his neck racing and pounding like a lone soldier who senses his end. "I will take you to your love," he repeated with a defeated flatness. "I will take you back in love."

## 34

After Baruch sealed the deed and buried it in Anatot, we began our journey back to Jerusalem. [2]Baruch was quiet, chipping at a block of chalk as we walked. He nudged an occasional mushroom with his toe and released a puff of spores, a tiny cloud of smoke. [3]I knew he was saddened. I squeezed his arm for him to stop. He lifted his head to me.

⁴I knelt onto the ground before him and I drew, in large letters, my name in the soil. ⁵I smiled up at him as I presented my offering, my name.

⁶"A-na-ti-ya," he read carefully. At last his sullen expression broke. ⁷"Anatiya! It is a beautiful name! 'God has answered me.' A beautiful meaning. Has God answered you?"

⁸I drew his name in the soil and gestured a question.

⁹He said, "Because my name means 'blessed,' you are asking me if God has blessed me?"

¹⁰I nodded.

"A good question. I look at myself next to many of my neighbors; I have my skill and my health, and I suppose I am blessed. ¹¹Then again, I look at myself next to my dreams . . . and in my dreams I have you, I mean, I really have you, and Babylon is just another foreign name with no bearing and no terror, and there are children around me with your glow and my smile," he blushed, "and then I don't feel so . . ."

¹²I put my arm around my friend and we walked. If my name had been a command . . . 'God! Answer me!' I would understand. ¹³But 'God has answered me' implies an acquired contentedness, which I have never, until perhaps, with this man, but not to the depth of me, not in my heart of hearts. ¹⁴Then again, my name could be a promise . . . etched into my gravestone . . . those distant generations will come to my tomb and say, "Anatiya. Indeed, God did answer her." ¹⁵Is that Your promise, God? Is that my destination? That my entire life be a question, and my death an answer? Your answer? ¹⁶God has answered me. ¹⁷God has answered *me*. ¹⁸I am God's answer.

¹⁹"Come, we'll turn in here for the night. There is an inn at the foot of the hills."

²⁰The twilight stars cooled the sky like a light winter frost. ²¹My arm draped in Baruch's arm felt gentle. Babylon melted. Jerusalem melted. Jeremiah blurred, his ranting muted. The orphans slept. My love quieted. ²²Evening was evening and nothing was more.

²³The innkeeper showed us to our room and Baruch paid him. ²⁴I lay myself upon the hard straw bed with my feet pulled up into my robes. Baruch stood quietly at the entrance looking at me. ²⁵He seemed so small just then, like a child, with a fragile frame and wide eyes. ²⁶I reached out my arms to him as I had done a thousand times for the orphans in the

street. ²⁷He said in a faraway voice, "My Master has not withheld anything from me in this house, except for you, for you are his wife." I smiled at this little Joseph. ²⁸He curled into my arms, and his musk comforted me to sleep.

²⁹In the late morning of the following day, Baruch led us off-course through the hills to a hidden spring. ³⁰We kicked off our sandals and ran to the pool. The cool water swallowed my legs and sent delightful zips and chills through my bones. ³¹Baruch thrust his whole head into the water, and came up laughing, with sunlit crystals flying off of his hair.

³²"Close your eyes for a moment!" he called to me. I closed them, delighting in the feel of the water between my toes. "You can open them now, but do not be afraid." ³³I opened my eyes and saw Baruch's brown body gleaming white under the sunlit water, his nakedness refracted by the wavelets into glimpses of a whole. ³⁴Baruch laughed and pointed at my face. "A sunrise in your cheeks!" he said. ³⁵I felt my cheeks and they were burning red. I narrowed my eyes at him, but the intentions of my heart were not cruel.

³⁶"Anatiya, come in. I shall not touch you." Baruch sucked in his breath and swam under the water. He emerged where the fresh water emerged from a crevice in the rocks. ³⁷He pressed his lips to the source and drank in long, luxurious drafts, and then let himself fall backwards into the sparkling pool. ³⁸Where was God in those moments? Where was the God of watching and judging? The God of wrath and condemnation? The sky was open and happy. The water was only inviting.

³⁹I lay my robes delicately upon the ground, and although I did not gesture for him to do so, Baruch turned away as I undressed. ⁴⁰I lay my skirt and unwrapped my sash, and I glided into the water. They swallowed me up to my neck in silky, cool brilliance. ⁴¹I let them swallow my head and my hair. I opened my eyes and looked at the muted light dancing on the bottom of the spring. ⁴²I saw Baruch's feet and legs dangling there and I came up for air. He was watching me and smiling and shining. ⁴³My toes found smooth rocks upon which to balance as I swam-walked-leapt-floated-danced to the source of the spring. ⁴⁴I lifted myself a bit out of the water and pressed my lips to the crevice in the rock. I had never tasted water so cold. ⁴⁵I could feel its wonderful chill down into my belly. I slipped back into the water. ⁴⁶Baruch and I stayed in the water for a long while,

always on opposite sides of the pool, but always with the other in the corner of our eye. ⁴⁷I emerged first and redressed over my wet skin, and then Baruch emerged and dressed. ⁴⁸In moments the heat dried us as we continued toward Jerusalem. ⁴⁹When we were close, Baruch squeezed my hand and said, "Babylon will tear down these walls very soon. We will go immediately to the Temple, where it will be safe, and where, too, I will bring you to your love." ⁵⁰A swoon came over my heart and a lovesickness took hold of my body. I leaned more heavily upon Baruch. I could feel Jeremiah near. ⁵¹My blood raced and the hair on my nape rose. A passion overcame me in wave of fever, and I could hear the blast of God's core, hosts of angels compressed into this one small city, and crying to be free. ⁵²I longed to see my prophet, while a part of me mourned for the morning's happy sky.

## 35

Baruch and I entered the House of the Lord in the evening, by the familiar orange glow of crackling fire. I withdrew my arm from his. ²There was a great hum in this place, as if a swarm of bees was near. It is You, God, condensed and trembling to fit in Your House.

³Jeremiah was seated at the head of a long table strewn with nibbled peels, little bones, and bread crumbs. ⁴A forest of goblets brimming with wine stood tall in the center of the table. Jeremiah's guests were the Rechabite people with their lean arms, long necks, and graceful, quiet gestures. ⁵They were licking their fingers and chattering politely with gentle smiles. Jeremiah lifted his tired eyes toward us and the weight of his weariness dropped upon me like a stone. ⁶He motioned us to sit beside him and said, "Have some wine."

⁷Baruch sat at my prophet's right hand, and I sat (or did the chair rise to meet me?) beside Baruch. I could feel, alternatively, a heat and a chill roll off of my prophet, as though the door to his heart were broken, swinging open and slamming shut. ⁸The goblets were all untouched, and it was clear to me that the Rechabites do not drink wine. ⁹I declined with eyes downcast. How could I pursue merriment while my love suffers so in my presence? ¹⁰I was flushed with shame at my frolicking with Baruch in Anatot. ¹¹Would that I had the courage and loyalty of Uriah when he said to the king: "Your majesty's men are camped in the open; how can

I go home and eat and drink and sleep with my wife?" [12]And yet, for an afternoon of sun and cool springs, wildflowers and this strange friend at my side, I abandoned my heart. [13]I love you, Jeremiah! I love you, slumped and sleepy prophet, how I love you. I will never again chase the wind.

[14]Baruch reached for a goblet of wine. He smiled at Jeremiah as he raised the goblet in thanks. [15]I was all too aware of the gulping of Baruch's throat as he drank one and two, three and four goblets. [16]I studied the deep-creased skin of my prophet, which appeared as aging parchment. [17]Baruch suddenly burst forth saying, "They say wine leads a man to sin! Isn't that so, Jeremiah? But isn't it also said that wine is the serum of truth, and it unlocks the lips and the secrets they protect." [18]Baruch looked at me with glazed eyes and slurred, "I have a secret to spill to you, Jeremiah."

[19]Jeremiah took hold of Baruch's arm and said sternly, "Do not say with your tongue what you would not write with your quill. There are truths too fragile to lance at with words." [20]Baruch was silenced and stared into his cup. [21]One by one, the Rechabites bowed before Jeremiah and kissed his hands as they took their leave. [22]I was terrified of the time when the last would have departed. Soon, we three were alone. [23]A pink haze of wine clung to Baruch and his head lolled from side to side. [24]While Jeremiah watched him absently, I watched with great dread, thinking, "Let the wine not overtake him, leaving me to fend my passion alone!"

[25]With a loud thud, Baruch's head hit the table. His eyes fluttered open from the pain, and locked onto me. [26]He smiled a crooked, loose smile, and said, "You see, my sweet? I have taken you to your love after all." [27]I stared at him stunned as his eyes rolled back and he began to snore. I will stare him awake, I thought, stare him awake with my anger. [28]How could he leave me alone with the prophet? I dared not look up.

[29]Then I heard Jeremiah speak the words slowly: "You ease my pain when I wear the yoke."

[30]I knew I had to be in a dream, hallucinating from the pink haze that clung to Baruch, and so the words did not penetrate my heart for a moment. [31]In my mind's eye, I looked at the words lightly, as if in a dream. [32]I wondered, matter-of-factly, why Jeremiah did not speak in the past tense . . . for it would be true to say that I *eased* his pain when he *wore* the yoke, when I rubbed melon-scented oil into his neck. [33]But an orator does not mistake his words. Perhaps he meant that I indeed ease his pain, that I comfort him when he bears the yoke of Heaven . . . [34]and then I was struck

in the heart that Jeremiah had indeed spoken! [35]That this is no dream, and he addressed me out loud! Out loud!

[36]I lifted my eyes, and indeed! My prophet was looking into them, steadily and even with . . . with . . . [37]what do I know of love? A mortal woman! Tears ran in sudden, unstoppable streams down my cheeks. He was looking at me. And speaking. [38]My love spoke to me:

"When Jacob saw Rachel,
he rolled the stone off the mouth of the well
and watered the flock
and then he kissed her.

[39]I have now seen the stone move off of the well.
I have now looked into the well.
[40]It is filled with the tears of Rachel's weeping.
I have now seen the waters that will water the flock.
[41]The living waters are your love.

[42]I was born with the stone on my soul,
a dislodged jewel
that seals my spirit as a pent-up fountain.
[43]I cannot love, for this stone.
[44]I cannot marry, for this stone.
[45]I cannot surrender, for this stone . . .
though with everything in me,
as God, my God lives,
I want . . .

[46]And no shepherd's strength,
and no king's command,
and no foreign force
could shift this stone.
[47]Even so,
I have now seen the stone move off of the well,
by the tiny splash of a woman's tear
and for a moment, with you, I am Jacob . . ."

[48]My love rose from the table, and his words were a net cast around my body, lifting me. I moved to him. [49]In an instant his arms locked around me, and he whispered and I felt the sweet breeze of his breath, [50]"I have never kissed, for this stone . . ." and I felt my lips press against my love. [51]I held tightly around his wide back and my tears streamed into our joined mouths. [51]All of the blood in me rushed in frenzy and every thought, every thought in the world, was silenced, every breath held, every wave on the sea, every tumbling rock, every star in its path stilled until . . . [52]My love pulled away, and his sweep of white hair smoothed over my neck, and he pressed his forehead to mine, and a white light pounded through the place our heads touched, and this light flooded my eyes. [53]I opened my mouth and said softly, but audibly, "I," and I cannot go on

and he said, "Hush, now, my bride. God returns."

# 36

The Lord descends over my prophet the way a gown falls over a maiden. [2]Jeremiah's God-armor is secure and he cannot interact with the mortal bride of his youth. He is bound in a sustained state of prophecy.

[3]Jeremiah dictated his poetry of looming disasters and Baruch wrote the words in a scroll. [4]I sat huddled in the shade with a certain peace in my heart, despite the sound of Jeremiah's lamentations. [5]I lovingly sharpened Baruch's quills and stitched his pages of parchment together. No matter how dire the words of wicked oppression, they cannot begin to squelch the little leaping sparks in me . . . [6]the sparks that dance in my heart like luminescent butterflies on sunlit fields. [7]An irrepressible smile flit across my lips when I considered . . . he kissed me!

[8]I lifted one of Baruch's quills and soaked its fine tip in ink. There is nothing, I thought, quite as thirsty as a quill. [9]I selected a trimming of parchment from the pile at my side and I wrote:

I love you.

[10]I looked at the words and I fell back a little. I was struck with a revelation that boxed my ears with truth. [11]The words that God once spoke to Moses and Israel, when He declared: "You shall love the Lord your God with all your heart, with all your spirit, and with all your might . . ." [12]I

suddenly understood the intent of these words. It is not a command, for how can one be commanded to love? Rather, I now know, it is a *promise*. [13]The supreme promise: You *shall* love. There will come a day when you shall love, and a day after that when *all* shall love, and *that* will be the waking day. [14]That will be the perfect age. Jeremiah had said, "I have now seen the waters that will water the flock. The living waters are your love." [15]The Messiah, the anointed one, will be resurrected through love. The Messiah will be love.

[16]At once I was filled with mission, and a spirit overtook me. An ecstasy came upon me. [17]I am reminded of the stories of Saul, when the Spirit of God came upon him, and he and his messengers stripped off their clothes and spoke in ecstasy. [18]Is this the Spirit of God upon me? I shiver in the heat without restraint. Am I, too, among the prophets? [19]The quill in my hand was a reed through which the wind of Heaven blew, and I wrote

> I love you
> I love you
> I love you
> I love you
> I love you
> I love you
> I love you
> I love
> I love
> I love

until I had filled all the trimmings of parchment with these words. [20]*This is how we will bring salvation . . . this is how the Messiah will be wakened and God's mercy roused . . . through love and only love.* [21]My hands searched for pebbles and rocks and I wrote the words upon them until I had filled a whole sack with these stones. I etched the words with a dry quill into bark.

[22]Jeremiah sent Baruch to the House of the Lord to read aloud the words from the scroll of Jeremiah's dictation. [22]Jeremiah was in hiding and could not preach in the House. I followed Baruch, bearing my sack

of trimmings and stones. ²³It was a day of fasting, and swarms of Judeans had come in to the Temple from the towns.

²⁴Baruch stood upon a step before the chamber of Gemariah in the upper court, near the gateway to the House of the Lord. ²⁵He stood upon a step, but his stature still seemed small. ²⁵He held the scroll before him, a shield between him and the people, and deepened his voice with found courage as he read the prophecy. ²⁶I tore a tiny hole in my sack and moved among the people, my stones and trimmings trailing behind, until the scroll was finished and the sack was empty.

²⁷I watched as people glimpsed down and considered, then stooped to pick up a note. ²⁸They glanced to and fro and then clutched it to their hearts. A woman secretly tucked it between her breasts. ²⁹A soldier dropped it into the hilt of his sword. Days later I will see these stones soldered into bracelets and rings all over the land.

³⁰Micaiah son of Gemariah heard Baruch read the scroll and he hurried to bring word to the king's official scribes. ³¹They sent for Baruch to bring the scroll. He told them, "The woman comes with me, too." And this way, I was brought to the palace.

³²As Baruch read the scroll to the scribes, my eyes drank in the room. Parchment hung drying from countless racks, covered with the fresh, formal writing of official records . . . ³³the advancement of Nebuchadrezzar's army, fortifications in the walls of Jerusalem and the palace gates, lists and lists of fallen soldiers, deposits to the treasuries, servants who have been released and others who have been hired, prisoners condemned and prisoners freed, royal births, deaths, and marriages. ³⁴On a table before me, a heavy, dusty scroll lay bound with an embroidered cloth which read "The Book of Kings." ³⁵Beside it stood a bottle of ink stopped with wax. As Baruch read the scroll and the scribes were transfixed, God forgive me, but my will overtook Your Spirit! ³⁶I slipped the bottle into my sack and a couple of quills beside.

³⁷When the reading of the scroll was complete, the scribes looked solemnly from one to the other. ³⁸They said, "Go into hiding, you and Jeremiah. Let no man know where you are!" ³⁹Baruch caught my eye as I slipped behind a curtain in the chamber. I will find out what will become of his scroll.

⁴⁰I followed the scribes to the king's winter palace. I pressed my cheek against the cold stone of a pillar as they gathered around the king's

furnace. ⁴¹They read to him the scroll, and every three or four columns, the king cut the scroll with a scribe's knife and threw it into the fire until the entire scroll was consumed. ⁴²The scribes protested the burning. They knew the scroll is the highest art, and their hearts were rent at its destruction. ⁴³They mourned the art of scroll, but not its truth, which they do not recognize. ⁴⁴I wept as I thought of Jeremiah's hoarse voice as he recited all of those words late through the night. I wept as I thought of Baruch hunched diligently over the parchment, endlessly recording in lovely letters, the moonlit prophecy. ⁴⁵I waited there weeping, until the burning was completed and the men retired to their chambers. ⁴⁶When the throne room was quiet, I slipped out like a shadow to the furnace. I gathered the ashes of the scroll into my sack and spirited them out of the palace.

⁴⁷In the open cool of evening, I thrust my hands deep into the ashes in the sack. This is the heart of my crushed prophet. ⁴⁸How dare they kindle the name of the living God! A spirit of ecstasy came upon me. There was a hum of God in my ears and a spark rising up through my feet. ⁴⁹I rubbed the ashes into my hair and into my cheeks. I smeared them across my brow. I shook the ashes of that scroll over my arms and rubbed them into my dress until the sack was empty, and I was covered in soot. ⁵⁰A charred alef was smeared over my eyelid. Other fragments of letters clung to my cool sweat like broken insect legs and wings. ⁵¹I walked toward the hiding place of Jeremiah and Baruch, with tears plowing long streaks through the soot on my face. I arrived at the cave in which they sat quietly by a fire.

⁵²I stood at the mouth of the cave with my arms lifted from my side, palms facing forward. Baruch leapt to his feet and cried, "Anatiya!"

But my eyes were fastened to Jeremiah. ⁵³For the first time, he seemed stunned . . . his eyes were wide. The whites of them glistened in the firelight. Lips parted. ⁵⁴Baruch rushed toward me, when Jeremiah spoke:

"Do not touch her, Baruch. She is wearing the scroll of God." ⁵⁵Jeremiah rose from his place. "She immersed herself in His words." ⁵⁶And he walked toward me, while Baruch remained frozen in his place. ⁵⁷"Dear prophetess," he said, as he stood close. "You are dark, but comely, O daughter of Jerusalem. Like the tents of Kedar . . . your locks are curled . . ." he entwined one around a thin, white finger, "and black as a raven, adorned with sapphires . . ." ⁵⁸Jeremiah softly stroked the side of my face, "Ashes to ashes, dust to dust."

⁵⁹"Jeremiah?" Baruch inquired. "Jeremiah, what is happening?"

[60]Jeremiah did not remove his eyes from mine, as my tears continued to well forth. [61]Jeremiah said, "This woman is called in life Anatiya. But the angels do call her Jerusalem. [62]Here before me, I see the whole city, fair Zion, fair and beautiful Zion, risen out of the ash-heap. [63]Baruch, open a blank scroll, and dip the quill in ink. Take down these words that I say. They shall call this scroll 'Lamentations.'"

[64]And as I stood before him, Jeremiah began to prophecy, with his eyes fastened to me . . . with his eyes gleaming and a fire in his brow . . . he spoke and Baruch wrote quickly to keep up, while I stood, weeping and upright and filthy before the prophet, poised like a model before an artist.

[65]Jeremiah spoke, and certain phrases clung to me, while others rolled away into the darkness:

[66]"Alas!
Bitterly she weeps through the night,
her cheeks wet with tears . . .
[67]uncleanness clings to her skirts . . .
[68]Zion spreads out her hands,
she has no one to comfort her . . .
the elders of fair Zion,
they have strewn dust on their heads . . .

[69]"Is this the city that was called Perfect in Beauty,
Joy of all the Earth?
[70]O wall of fair Zion,
shed tears like a torrent day and night,
give yourself no respite,
your eyes no rest,
pour out your heart like water . . .

[71]"I am the man who has known God's wrath . . .
He has ground me into dust . . .

[72]"But this do I call to mind,
and therefore I have hope,

it is good for a man, when young, to bear a yoke,

let him put his mouth to the dust,

there may yet be hope.

[73]For the Lord does not reject forever,

first afflicts,

then pardons in His abundant kindness.

[74]Let us search and examine our ways,

and turn back to the Lord.

[75]Let us lift up our hearts with our hands to God in Heaven.

[76]"We have transgressed and rebelled,

and You have not forgiven,

[77]You have slain without pity,

You have made us filth and refuse in the midst of the peoples . . .

[78]"My eyes shall flow without cease,

until the Lord looks down and beholds from Heaven.

[79]My eyes have brought me grief over all the maidens of my city.

[80]The guilt of my poor people . . .

her elect were purer than snow, whiter than milk,

now their faces are blacker than soot . . .

our skin glows like an oven with fever of famine . . .

[81]"Turn us back O Lord, to Yourself, and lift us out of the ash heap!"

[82]At last Jeremiah collapsed to his knees, utterly spent. In his hands, he clutched my skirts. [83]He buried his head into the folds of my robes and sobbed. Baruch lay down his quill. [84]He looked frightened as he approached us. He touched Jeremiah's back lightly and said, "You have, if I may, my lord sir, let me fetch water under cover of darkness that you may bathe, my lord, please, if I may."

[85]"Let the city bathe," Jeremiah's words were muffled in my skirt. "Let Jerusalem be cleansed."

[86]Baruch hurried to bring water. He was gone for a long while, and all throughout, Jeremiah clutched my legs and sobbed, "O Jerusalem."

## 37

I looked down upon Jeremiah. The Lord had dropped a cage over my mind. No thought could penetrate. <sup>2</sup>I saw the prophet, his white flowing hair . . . I saw him as if from a long distance. I saw him clutching my legs, but I could not feel him. <sup>3</sup>My legs were numb from standing. Even so, from this distance, my love rushed out to him, and my heart beat with such speed . . . <sup>4</sup>perhaps I am dying.

<sup>5</sup>Baruch materialized out of the dark. He tapped Jeremiah and said, "My lord, please come, I have prepared a bath." <sup>6</sup>He led Jeremiah to the back of the cave, where he had prepared a basin of water ensconced by two oil lamps. <sup>7</sup>Jeremiah let fall his robe and slipped, without a ripple, into the water. <sup>8</sup>Baruch returned to my side, and his face still looked frightened.

<sup>9</sup>He lightly touched the backs of my knees and at once they unlocked and bent. <sup>10</sup>I crumpled to the ground in a cloud of black dust and I let him hold me to his chest. <sup>11</sup>Baruch rocked me, and he softly chanted a childhood song:

> "Fill your mouth with honeycomb
> and sweet grapes from the vine
> only don't talk now, troubled one,
> don't open your mouth for talking.
> <sup>12</sup>Let the sweet in,
> but let no sorrow out.
> I'll let no sorrow out,
> for I'll stop it up with sweet."

<sup>13</sup>I found myself on the brink of sleep. The tears were dried and cracking on my face. <sup>14</sup>Baruch stroked my hair as we lay in a heap on the ground. <sup>15</sup>We heard Jeremiah's voice above us say: "Let Jerusalem bathe."

<sup>16</sup>Baruch helped me to my feet and walked me to the same bath in which Jeremiah had bathed. <sup>17</sup>Was I to immerse my naked self in the place where my prophet had washed? I looked to Baruch and he turned away. <sup>18</sup>I watched as he and Jeremiah exited the cave that I might be alone. I stared into the dark waters and the flicking candlelight they reflected. <sup>19</sup>I felt a great sense of awe, as if I was standing before the very source

of all life. A forbidden fountain of youth. [20]I let my robes drop to the ground and I stepped cautiously into the waters. [21]Slowly, they swallowed me ... my legs and my hips, my breasts and my shoulders ... I poured cupfuls over my face and I lowered my hair. [22]I loosened the soot and untangled my hair with my fingers. My legs were bent and my knees were two gleaming summits. [23]I felt the waters seeping inside of me. I clenched the waters inside, that the waters my love and I shared might become a true part of me.

[24]When I emerged, I wrapped myself in a new robe Baruch had laid out before the bath. Overwhelmed by fatigue, I curled on a mat and faded into night.

[25]I woke to the smell of sweet flowers. My head felt cool, as my hair was still damp, and my body felt happy and refreshed. [26]My eyes peeled slowly open, and here was Baruch holding a bouquet of wildflowers beneath my nose. [27]I smiled at him. He said, "That scroll that you inspired, Anatiya. I read it this morning. It is so beautiful, so profound, filled with such pain and longing, I ..."

[28]I glanced about the cave in the dusty shafts of early sunlight. Baruch followed my eyes. [29]He said, "Jeremiah has come out of hiding. The wrath of God is in him, and he cannot remain in this place."

[30]I sat upright and worry overtook me. Baruch looked down. "The king is very angry with him. I tried to stop him, but that fire, you know, that fire was in him, and I could not get close." [31]He studied my face for a pause. Then he extended his hand and helped me from the ground. "Come, Jerusalem, we will find him together."

[32]When we found Jeremiah, he was in the house of the scribe Jonathan, which had been made into a jail. [33]He was covered in bruises and welts, and clumps of his hair were missing. The jail cell was dark and dank, with a terrible odor. [34]There was only a tiny slot for a window. His eyes through that slot were red with crying.

"Jeremiah!" cried Baruch. "Who put you in this place!"

[35]"A man named Fear," my prophet replied. His eyes turned to me, as I stood a little back, my face peeking over Baruch's shoulder. [36]Jeremiah suddenly burst into loud and dreadful sobbing. He howled, "Please hear me, and grant my plea! Don't leave me in here to die!"

[37]The pain of his plea pierced my heart and I collapsed on the stone pavement. Baruch gathered me in his arms and took me to a shady place. [38]He patted me on the cheeks and roused me to wakefulness. [39]He said to

me, "He will remain in the prison a long time, sweet bride. They will not let him go. ⁴⁰I have spoken with many officials on his behalf. The best we can do is bring him bread to eat from the Baker's Street until all the bread in the city is gone. ⁴¹We will bring him water, and you will bring him hope. And we will keep him alive."

38

Baruch and I scavenged the city for bread, and it became increasingly difficult to find. ²There were corpses littering the streets. I stared into their young faces, gaunt with a hunger that was never satiated. ³Somewhere some mother gave birth to these fallen souls . . . some mother had suckled them, hoped for them, dreamed for them, and here they lay strewn about the city. ⁴I carried with me my stolen ink and quills. I closed the eyelids of the corpses, that the sun not burn out their flat eyes. ⁵I wrote on their eyelids, "I love you." They were my parchment.

⁶As I scavenged for bread one late afternoon, a creeping sensation came over me. I spun around, and there before me was the child Ezekiel, gleaming in health, his face the face of an angel with eyes pale as sky and hair white-gold. ⁷With him was standing a man, taller than any I had ever seen. The lean giant was clad in white linen, with a writing case hanging at his side. ⁸His face was enveloped in sun so that I could not make out its features. Ezekiel embraced me and I wept in his arms. He reached into his robe and removed a loaf of bread for me.

⁹"Listen, sister Zion, you are not to give this loaf to Jeremiah. Give him what you yourself scavenge, but keep this loaf for yourself." ¹⁰Ezekiel lay his hands upon my belly and smiled. "You know, virgin Zion, that you are with child. Your love will bring forth a son."

¹¹I thought in my mind, "How is this possible?" The spirit of Sarah laughed inside me. I have not even been with a man!

¹²Ezekiel, who understood my thoughts, answered, "When you came to the husband of your soul, covered in soot and ash, your beauty shined out to him stronger than the sun. ¹³His love for you then filled him with a passion that tore through his heart in a great rush of emotion. ¹⁴O that I should find a love so strong! His love poured forth in painful prophecy, a scroll that was torn from the deepest chamber of his heart. ¹⁵When he immersed in his bath, his love poured forth again . . . not in words, not in

poetry, for his mouth and God were silent. His love poured forth into the bath. [16]You remember, lovely Jerusalem, when you stood before the bath in which the husband of your soul had bathed, you were afraid and filled with awe. You felt you were standing before the very source of all life. [17]You immersed, and the essence of his love filled you." Ezekiel caressed my belly. "You shall have a child by Jeremiah."

[18]A great trembling overtook me and rattled me to the bone. A great sense of fear filled my heart. That God should play with me so! [19]That this exquisite child Ezekiel should see into time, see into past and future with such vivid clarity . . . [20]that God should consider me worthy to bear the child of a prophet, of the prophet I have stalked and loved and who made me sick with desire, could it be true? [21]But the truth of it had already seized me at the neck and sent shudders of terror through my bones. [22]Who am I, O Lord? Who am I? A shattered urn, a forgotten dream . . . who am I but flesh and blood, to carry out Your designs?

[23]Ezekiel squeezed my hand. "You are loved, fair Zion, from within and without. And your love shall bring Israel back to the land. [24]And your love shall redeem this people. And your love shall summon up miracles. I praise the love in you, prophetess, just as I praise the God of love."

[25]The man in linen who accompanied Ezekiel removed a quill from his writing case. He bent down and drew a mark upon my forehead. [26]The touch of his quill released a certain peace in me. I inquired in my mind about the man in linen.

[27]Ezekiel responded, "He is an angel of the Lord, silent like you. Although," Ezekiel smiled, "I am aware that you did speak a single word, and it crashed through the heavens like a meteor." [28]He continued, "Soon, God's wrath will dispatch the angels of death, and they will slay all those whose brows are not marked. [29]You now wear the mark which is invisible to mortals, but a bright adornment to the realms of Heaven. [30]We must hurry now, Zion, for there are others we must seek . . . sadly, though, the numbers are few." [31]The child and angel departed, and I looked after them, clutching the aromatic bread to my breast.

[32]Word came to Baruch that a band of priests and officials were urging the king to execute Jeremiah. [33]They said, "Let that man be put to death, for he disheartens the soldiers, and all the people who are left in this city." [34]We rushed to the prison to see the men lowering Jeremiah by ropes into the pit of Malchiah. [35]We stood at the edge of the pit. Jeremiah's head was bowed heavily as they lowered him down. He did not look up to see us.

[36]He sank at the bottom of the pit into mud that reached his waist. There was no food and no water, and he could not sit and rest lest he drown in the mud. [37]His appearance was so forlorn, he was but a shell of himself. I flung myself at one of the guards who was holding the ropes. [38]I clutched at his garments and wept before him. Baruch raised his voice in angry protest, but the men shooed us away like little pests. [39]I lay at the edge of the pit with my face hanging over and my tears falling into the mud like coins into a wishing well. [40]All at once I was seized with a thought. I took from Baruch a trimming of parchment and wrote upon it:

You have conceived a child, my only love. God's blessing upon us all.

[41]I let the leaf flutter into the pit. I saw by a turn of my prophet's head that the note caught his eye as it rested, face-up, on the mud. [42]He read it slowly, and without his looking up, and I saw the power and the truth of its words strike him. [43]He pressed the note to his brow and bellowed and wailed. His imprisonment was unbearable to him, and he cried out to God with a great and sudden fury in his upraised fist. [44]His anger took me by surprise. He cried out:

"Why do You love to confuse me?
Why do You throw me in the deepest pit
to starve, to anguish, and to die a slow death?
[45]Why do You torment me so that I am sure that You hate me,
and then suddenly, as I anguish,
You extend Your hand in love and You tell me You love me."

[46]Jeremiah looked up to the sky and his rage seared past me and threw me back.

[47]"Why, God!
Why do You turn me in this way only to turn me in that?
Why do You twist me so that confusion grips my soul!
[48]Do You love me?
Then why do You pursue me with vengeance?
Do You hate me?"
He peeled the note from his brow and shook it at the sky.

"Then why do you tempt me with joy?"

⁴⁹Jeremiah continued with mud sputtering from his lips and a hoarseness in his shouting.

"Is it enough, do You think,
while I sink in the mud,
while my stomach is hollow,
to let me see the smallest circle of sky and send me this sliver of
    hope?
⁵⁰This glimpse at a future while I lay here
wallowing and suffering to the root of my soul?
Is it enough, do You think, to sustain me?

⁵¹"You have robbed me of everything!
You have robbed me of youth!
⁵²You have robbed me of the love of a woman!
You have made me a laughingstock among the people!
A thing to jeer at!
⁵³Why did You create me? To torment?
Why do You give life and then make man despise it?
⁵⁴And now,
though You have robbed me of intimacy with the bride of my youth,
now You give me a son,
just to rob me again!

⁵⁵"And You think it is enough to sustain a man?
A little sky? An offspring?
Is this Your offering to me?
⁵⁶It is not enough!
It is not enough, God!
It is not enough!
⁵⁷Let him die in his mother's womb as I should have died!
O that my father never conceived me!
⁵⁸Why do You send jackals to tear at me limb from limb?
Let me go, Lord!

Let me be!

How can I be Your servant when You torture me so?

[59]"This!"—

he shook the note in his fist at the heavens—

"This is not enough!"

[60]Jeremiah threw himself against the side of the pit and I could hear his muffled cries into the mud. [61]"My feet have sunk in the mire. You have sent me alive into Sheol. And now You have sent me alive into Sheol. Let me be!"

[62]There was a eunuch in the king's palace named Ebed-melech who heard the shouting of Jeremiah, and his heart was wrenched for the prophet. [63]He spoke to the king, saying, "O lord king, those men have acted wickedly in all they did to the prophet Jeremiah. They have put him down in the pit, to die there of hunger." [64]The compassion of Ebed-melech roused mercy in the king and he instructed the servant to pull the prophet out of the pit. [65]Ebed-melech (God bless his name forever!) told the guards to lower the ropes. [66]Ebed-melech (to the thousandth generation, God bless his kind name!) tore the shirt off his back. His muscular skin shone like sapphire. [67]He tossed the shirt into the pit and called to Jeremiah, "Put the worn cloths and rags under your armpit, inside the ropes, that your skin does not bruise and chafe." Jeremiah did so.

[68]When they pulled him up, he was like a limp weed torn from the earth. When they placed him on the ground, his legs gave out from fatigue and misery. [69]His skin was ghostly white striped with pale blue lines. Old bruises were green stains with faded yellow edges. His lips were cracked from thirst. [70]A circle of guards surrounded him and taunted his appearance. [71]I sat crumpled onto the ground as Baruch tried to wedge his way to Jeremiah. [72]I peered Ebed-melech walking away, head bent, rubbing his eyes. I leapt up and ran to him. [73]I stood in his path and took his broad and beautiful face in my hands. I kissed his salty eyelids and held him for a long while. [74]He said to me, "I can feel we are near the end."

[75]I left him on his way and returned to find Baruch consoling Jeremiah. The guards had become bored and abandoned their mockery. [76]Out of the heap which was Jeremiah, I saw a bony arm reach out, and a near skeletal hand extend. I heard Jeremiah whisper, "Come, O Jerusalem."

⁷⁷I rushed to my love in a flurry of robes and tears, and threw my arms about him.

⁷⁸In that moment, Jerusalem was captured.

# 39

In the ninth year of King Zedekiah of Judah, in the tenth month, King Nebuchadrezzar of Babylon moved against Jerusalem with his whole army. ²On the ninth day of the fourth month, the walls of the city were breached. ³Baruch, Jeremiah, and I remained in the prison compound. ⁴We knew that Jeremiah was too weak to leave, and Baruch made claim that the compound was the safest place in the city at that time.

⁵In the middle of the night, King Zedekiah and all of his soldiers fled the city by way of the king's garden. ⁶Baruch and I had wrapped Jeremiah in goatskins to keep him warm. ⁷I set a hot kettle of tea beside him. The steam brought moisture and a faint glow to his blanched pallor. ⁸His weary eyes were set in deep, dark circles. We had left Jeremiah in his sullen state to search for food, when we heard the clamor and clinking of battle gear. ⁹Baruch and I sat amidst the flowerbeds of the king's garden and watched as the soldiers and officials fled. ¹⁰"They will not escape," Baruch said to me. ¹¹And then he stood up before I could stop him and yelled, "You will all die, just as Jeremiah predicted! You are marching to your death!"

¹²The soldiers looked over at Baruch. I feared for a moment that they would kill him. But then I saw in their faces a white veil of dread. They moved on.

¹³Baruch and I entered the palace. The halls were wide and empty, lined in beautiful textured and painted stone. ¹⁴Tapestries depicting battles hung from the walls. I studied them. The battles were unfamiliar to me. ¹⁵Perhaps the tapestries were looted from foreign lands, or brought to King Solomon in ages past on the Queen of Sheba's chariots.

¹⁶"Come here!" I heard Baruch call.

¹⁷I followed his voice to the center of the palace into the throne room. I laughed when I entered. ¹⁸Baruch was sitting upon the throne! "Come! It is wide enough for the two of us!" I joined him upon the throne and we surveyed the majestic court. ¹⁹He put his arm around me lightly. ²⁰He said, "You know, my dear woman, that outside these walls is a great slaughter. That blood is flowing out into the streets with no end. While we are living like king and queen!"

²¹After he spoke, a sadness fell upon us both and upon the expansive court before us. ²²He turned to me and said, "Is it true that you are with child?" I nodded yes.

²³"Then it is true that the walls of Jerusalem have been breached!" He exclaimed and leapt out of the throne. He began dancing an awkward sort of dance about the court. ²⁴"I'm a jester!" he called. "A jester for the queen of Jerusalem!"

²⁵Just then a shadow appeared from behind a pillar. ²⁶The shadow spoke, "I can feel that the dead are all around." ²⁷Baruch froze in his place and the shadow stepped forward. It was Ebed-melech. ²⁸I hurried to him from the throne and took his large hands in mine. ²⁹He smiled faintly at me and said, "I can feel it everywhere. The slaying, the fresh blood. The women of the city have shackles around their necks. ³⁰They are being transported to Babylon as slaves. The Temple treasuries have been raided . . . blood on the Temple steps. ³¹The altar fire is just smoke and ash. A priest's severed hand. ³²And the soldiers, they have a bloodlust for children . . . the screaming. The screaming! ³³I can't seem to . . . this death, it makes the whole city sag. The walls are in heaps. There are children crushed underneath!"

³⁴Baruch lay his hand on Ebed-melech's shoulder to comfort him. We led him to sit on the throne to calm him. ³⁵He continued:

"I saw it with my own eyes. The Chaldean troops pursued my lord King Zedekiah. They overtook him on the steppes of Jericho. ³⁶They slaughtered each of his children before his eyes, dashing the little ones against a rock! ³⁷Then they massacred all the nobles of Jerusalem. This death . . . this death is all around! ³⁸They gouged out the eyes of my lord king and led him in chains to Babylon." Ebed-melech bolted upright. ³⁹He said, "They will come here next! Let us go to the prison compound where we will be safe!"

⁴⁰Ebed-melech started to run, but Baruch grabbed hold of him. "We need food."

⁴¹Ebed-melech took our hands and rushed us to the king's pantries. We filled our arms with scraps of bread and grain, and ran to the compound. ⁴²There we found Jeremiah fast asleep. I nuzzled against his side, for God's Presence had lifted from him, and we waited for the Chaldeans to arrive.

## 40

Ebed-melech roused the three of us from sleep. ²He thrust handfuls of bread and grain into our laps and said, "Eat quickly, they are here." ³We ate the bread in half-chewed swallows. I pushed morsels into Jeremiah's lips and he chewed them delicately. ⁴Outside the compound we heard a great shout. "They have set the palace on fire," said Ebed-melech mournfully. ⁵He cast his eyes to the ground. "I have lived there since I was a boy. Now I have no home."

⁶Baruch put his arm around him. "You will stay with us, if you wish. Tell me, young man, where was it that you were born?"

⁷"Ethiopia," Ebed-melech replied.

⁸"Why don't you sing us a song of your true home, to help ease our minds."

⁹Ebed-melech stood up and began to sing a mournful, soulful ballad in a lisping foreign tongue. ¹⁰As he sang, behind him the palace windows burst into flame. Tears welled in his eyes as his singing become more passionate. ¹¹Every ache in his heart was poured into that foreign melody, and we all sat at his feet listening to a language we did not know, but a sentiment we well understood.

¹²As the song ended, soldiers began to comb the compound. They burst into the cell in which we were hiding, but none of us jumped or became afraid, for the song of Ebed-melech had so deeply calmed our souls. ¹³If they had killed me then, I would have been ready. I would not have asked God to answer why.

¹⁴But they did not kill us. They chained us in fetters and led us by torchlight amidst all those from Jerusalem and Judah who were being exiled to Babylon. ¹⁵I struggled to walk in the fetters, to keep up with Jeremiah and Ebed-melech. ¹⁶My prophet had suddenly regained strength. He walked erect and with purpose. ¹⁷Dear Lord! Do not let me become lost in this swarm of chained people and disappear in the valley of Babylon! ¹⁸Baruch saw my struggle and moved behind me so that he might gently push me along and steady me when I stumbled. ¹⁹We walked until the soles of my sandals wore off. ²⁰Jeremiah seemed stronger and stronger . . . his lips, I observed, were almost smirking. This is the day that he knew would soon come.

²¹When we arrived at Ramah, an Israelite in fetters was being led from group to group by a Chaldean soldier. ²²When he arrived at the four of us, he pointed at Jeremiah and said, "Here! This is the one you want!"

²³The soldier shouted something in his language to summon others. A soldier appeared with an air of authority. ²⁴He wore a tall, gleaming helmet adorned with a plume. His uniform was decorated with silver, brass, and gold. The other soldiers parted before him. ²⁵He walked to Jeremiah and spoke in Hebrew:

"I am Nebuzaradan, the chief of the guards. Are you the prophet Jeremiah?"

"As God lives."

²⁶"King Nebuchadrezzar, long may he reign! has ordered me to look after you and grant you what you desire. ²⁷The Lord Your God threatened the place with disaster, and now the Lord has brought it about. ²⁸The people sinned, and that is why this has happened. We know that you prophesied that the people should surrender to the king of Babylon, lest tragedy befall them. They did not pay heed. This we know. ²⁹Now, I release you from these fetters. If you would like to go with me to Babylon, come, and I will look after you, for you are a great and inspired prophet. ³⁰Or, you can go to Gedaliah, whom the king of Babylon has put in charge of the towns of Judah, and stay with him among the people. Or go wherever you want to go, wherever seems right to you."

³¹"I will go to Gedaliah, and I will take my three disciples with me."

³²The guards released us from our fetters and brought us to Gedaliah at Mizpah.

³³"You all look tired and dirty!" the wife of Gedaliah exclaimed. "Sit down and I will bring water to wash your feet." ³⁴We had not slept in a long while and we collapsed onto a stone bench. ³⁵Only Jeremiah remained standing, surveying our surroundings. ³⁶My eyes were too bleary with exhaustion to take anything in. Around my ankles and wrists were blisters and sores from where the fetters had been. ³⁷The wife of Gedaliah returned with a basin of water and some cloth. She knelt and washed the feet of Jeremiah. ³⁸I lost consciousness on Baruch's shoulder.

³⁹I awoke when I felt my feet slip into water. Baruch and Ebed-melech had had their feet cleaned, and now it was my turn. ⁴⁰I watched as from a great distance as the wife of Gedaliah methodically washed my feet. Her

firm grip was comforting as was her determined scrubbing. [41]When she was finished she laid out before us a trayful of bread, figs, and grapes all drizzled with honey and goblets of wine. [42]We gratefully devoured all she laid before us. When the tray was removed, her husband Gedaliah entered to greet us. [43]He had the strength and build of a champion warrior, but his face retained a certain innocence in contrast with his muscles and scars. He embraced Jeremiah.

[44]"I have a house already prepared for you, Jeremiah. It is so good, and I thank God you are here! Anything you ask, my lord, and I will seek to provide."

[45]"I ask that the Lord leave this remnant in peace."

[46]"A tall order!" laughed a jovial Gedaliah. "Wife! See to it ... if God should come to our door, let him know that His prophet is busy!"

[47]The wife of Gedaliah looked afraid. She said sternly, "God is welcome in this home, and he who says otherwise shall be cursed." Thereupon she spit three times on the floor.

[48]Gedaliah laughed, "Of course, of course. Everyone is welcome! Come, my friends, let me show you the house I have prepared for you."

# 41

Gedaliah led us to a small two-room stone house. A neat little fire danced in the main room, surrounded by fluffy sheepskin mats.

[2]"There is a second room in which the woman can rest, if she desires," Gedaliah said. [3]We thanked him and soon after he left, we were all asleep in the soft wool ... [4]while the exiles were marched to a foreign land, and the palace of the king burned, while the cold of night crept over the corpses piled in the town square, we were nested in softness and warmth. And we felt, strangely, perhaps heretically, guiltless.

[5]I do not know where God's Presence was in the months to follow. Perhaps He escorted the exiles to distant lands. [6]I uncovered little glimpses of God as I tended a garden behind the house ... in the blush of a fig, in the sweetness of a bundle of grapes ... [7]I saw God's fingerprints in the soil at the change of the season, and I felt God's kindness, God's promise to plant and not to uproot, as I felt my belly stretch and grow. [8]This was a God I remembered from my infancy, a God of wonder and nature that I knew and loved, before language interfered ... [9]a God Who embraced

me in the sweetened heat that rose off of a field of grain, Who made the constellations turn and the moon wane and the water wet, [10]and gave everything essence, made everything unique . . . the barley stalk different from the wheat stalk, the ox different from the mule, and me different from . . . [11]This was the God of Being, not Doing . . . without wrath or command or judgment. [12]This part of God was mute like me and I communicated with this part of God best.

[13]Jeremiah spent much of each day sitting in the garden as I worked the soil. Sometimes he bent down to sift the soil in his hands, to bring it to his nose and smell its aroma. [14]He and I, our shoulders became bronzed. The sun streaked my hair gold and the little hairs on my arms and legs as if I had stepped out of a cloud of gold dust. [15]Jeremiah seemed healthy. His hair shined and his eyes were bright. His back was straight . . . he was no longer wracked with God's angry torrents. [16]Where had God's Presence gone? Did He heed Jeremiah's pain when my prophet shouted from the pit, "Let me be!" [17]Had He discarded Jeremiah, had He no longer any use of a vessel, now that Jerusalem was captured and the slaughter complete? [18]And if Jeremiah was no longer His prophet, then what of my love for Jeremiah the man?

[19]It is no longer a desperate sort of love that makes me swoon and sick in the heart. And yet it is not less. O no, it is more. [20]It is a love that comes out of health and not sickness, out of understanding and not obsession. [21]It is a love face-to-face, man-to-woman. And I find him more beautiful than ever . . . his deep gray eyes creased at the corners from so many righteous tears, the thickness of his hands with which he wrestled so many sorrows, the softness of his tongue and his lips that had formed too many jagged sharp words, [22]his ample thighs that were once so lean and carried him across this land from top to bottom, his shoulders that he lets droop in a defiant laziness hard won . . . [23]his whole body is a map of journeys completed, and I love this easy softness we share.

[24]He hardly speaks, but when he does, he strikes a chime in my heart and a blush rises to my cheeks.

[25]"I love to share your quietness," he will say as he sits in the sun, husking wheat.

[26]One night, as I burrowed into my sheepskin mats, Jeremiah came to me for the first time. He sat beside me and started to speak. The words, it seemed, were difficult for him to form . . . they had been pent-up for so long:

²⁷"I always knew, Jerusalem,
that you were there,
peering into my window,
lurking in the shadow.
²⁸I could smell the tangy sweetness of your skin,
I could feel the heat in your hair,
in its wonderful waves.
²⁹I stole a glimpse of you . . .
your crimson lips shone like olive oil,
and your eyes were the only eyes,
the only eyes that saw everything,
³⁰they drank in visions like quills drinking ink.
³¹I saw the swell of your breasts
and the fullness of your hips . . .
³²I watched you age with me,
as a wine growing richer and riper each season.
³³And I could not turn to you,
for my soul was attached to God,
my spirit in the grip of His right hand.
³⁴He held me on the brink of Sheol
and afflicted me with His breakers.
³⁵But His hand has lifted from me,
and at last I am unfettered
to fulfill a mortal gladness,
to drink from my own cistern
and find joy in the wife of my youth,
a loving doe . . .
³⁶and behold,
you are still here!
³⁷You have never left my side,
a loyal and faithful bride
to the very end.
³⁸How I feared I would lose you,
your presence is a healing salve.
³⁹Many women have done well,

but you, Jerusalem, surpass them all."

⁴⁰Jeremiah gathered me in his arms. He bent his face toward me and I
lifted mine to his, but before he kissed me, there arose a need in him to
add:

⁴¹"I love God,
I do.
With all my heart
and all my soul
and all my might.
⁴²But let me, this once,
love God through you."

⁴³He kissed me and a fire consumed me. I felt the blood drain completely
from my face only to return in a burning rush. ⁴⁴He pulled me into his lap
and we pressed into each other, and banners were raised in my thought,
declaring: This is the body of my prophet! This is his taste and his touch!
⁴⁵This is the Garden of Eden, hanging with luscious fruits and brilliant with
ever-flowing streams! ⁴⁶This is the one my heart has sought through every
city square and every sand-strewn path, here in my arms, in his arms, this
is the prophet Jeremiah, this is Jeremiah the man . . . a part of me, and I a
part of him. ⁴⁷His sealed eyelids were dewy and pearlescent. ⁴⁸His hair was
a curtain of white silk that fell over my shoulders in cool cascades. ⁴⁹His
kisses upon my neck were prayers of gratitude, offerings of thanksgiving, his
embrace worshipful. ⁵⁰This was the love that I knew lay dormant, hidden at
the core of his volcanic God-fervor, the love that I prayed to blossom. My
careful tending. ⁵¹He kissed and caressed and clung to me, and I cried and
quivered until there was no border between my tears and his, no boundary
between trembling, no fence between reverence and rapture, life and death
and resurrection and death again, to which the choirs of Heaven and earth
cry "Amen, selah!" for rebirth, which is as certain as dawn is to break. ⁵²And
we lay, gleaming and wet in each other's arms, soft and warm as melted wax,
and the breath of my prophet was deep and even and easy, and the child I
carried turned in my womb.

## 42

As I lay in Jeremiah's arms, he said to me: "Gedaliah, God bless him, he is a good and trusting man. But his downfall is this: He thinks the war is over." ²Indeed, in the seventh month, King Baalis of Ammon sent one of his commanders along with ten men to kill Gedaliah at Mizpah because of his loyalty to the king of Babylon. ³Jeremiah, Baruch, Ebed-melech, and I were working in the garden before the heat of the day ⁴when we heard the voice of Gedaliah call out loudly: "Wife! Run and fetch our guests some water. O no! It is no trouble at all, take off your battle gear and sit. There is no need for swords here."

⁵A moment later we heard the shattering of vessels and the high shrieking of Gedaliah's wife.

⁶"This is it," Ebed-melech leapt to his feet. "Come quickly, there is an empty cistern in which you may hide." ⁷We followed the good Ebed-melech as he led us to an empty cistern just outside the town. Jeremiah, Baruch, and I hurried down into its depths and Ebed-melech, ever loyal servant, rushed back to the home of Gedaliah. ⁷We sat in the cool darkness utterly silent as the shouts increased from the land above. We stayed there all the day and night.

⁸On the second day, we heard the rebels coming closer to the mouth of the cistern. We huddled into the farthest corner as they approached. ⁹All at once—O God! Erase this terror from my eyes!—a body was thrown into the cistern, landing, headfirst with a terrible crack, in a twisted heap. ¹⁰I clutched Jeremiah and Baruch beside me for fear. Only moments after another slain soul was tossed down. They are using this cistern as a mass unmarked tomb! ¹¹The bodies, all men, kept falling in a terrible torrent. I felt my heart was ripped out and a terrible fear flooded me. ¹²Are we to be buried alive? O God! Shall this be my grave, and shall my womb be a grave for my child? ¹³Dear Lord Almighty God, is this the price for a few months respite? I know I am guilty, O Heaven! I lured your chosen prophet into my arms. ¹⁴Do not punish us on account of my sin! I wept as the bodies rained down. ¹⁵Living God! Here lies the remnant of Israel! Their blood is fresh and their bodies are warm and their stench of fear fills the air around me. ¹⁶I bury me head in my robes to hide them from my view. It seems ages before I recognize Baruch's arm cradling me, and his voice speaking: "It has stopped, Anatiya. There are no more for now. It has

stopped." [17]He turns to Jeremiah and I hear him ask, "Jeremiah, what does your God say to us now?" [18]Jeremiah just rocks in his place. I wipe the tears from my eyes and see for the first time that he is as trauma-stricken as I. He is ghostly pale and shaken. [19]I am ashamed that in the presence of such death, my sorrow gives way to a selfish thought. [20]I wonder, (forgive my arrogance and lofty self-regard!) "Does he regret his time with me? Does he blame me? Does he feel that I stained and soiled his linen-white bond with God?" [21]And how can I think of myself at this time? Me! A mortal woman with no voice . . . [22]if only I knew where in my body my ego rests, I would promptly cut it out and stamp it into dust! [23]Through the tremors in Jeremiah's teeth he responds to Baruch saying: "God says nothing to me. He is closed, closed up as the grave. God says nothing to me."

[24]"We must move the bodies and make room, that we may get out," Baruch repeated to Jeremiah as he untangled the bodies and layered them along the sides of the cistern. [25]"Jeremiah," he repeated, "help me move the bodies." With great effort, Jeremiah lifted himself and joined Baruch. [26]All the while he muttered prayers, "Do not, O Lord, annihilate the remnant of Israel. For the sake of our ancestors, for the sake of Your Name, do not, O Lord, wipe them out, every one."

[27]When at last we climbed out of the pit, I threw my head back before the star-splayed sky. [28]Praised be God for the night! Under cover of darkness, my life feels secure. And that sprinkle of sparkling light—a sun every one, but distant as Heaven—they soothe me with their purity and comfort me with their steady course. [29]O cool and forgiving night, lift up all those slain spirits and usher them swiftly into Eden!

[30]We washed our bodies with well-water. Jeremiah scrubbed his skin as if the corpses had contaminated him (as if, God forbid, he thought I contaminated him?) and his skin was red and raw. [31]We returned to the little house that the good man Gedaliah had given us, and found that it had not been touched. [32]Baruch built a fire and the three of us sat staring into it. I stared until I started to detect patterns in the flame, how the dance of the blue flame was sensually slow, and the orange whipped itself up and then back, and the red . . . all at once Ebed-melech snapped us out of our spell.

[33]"My lord Jeremiah!" he cried, breathless, "Johanan son of Kareah, and all the officers with him, heard of the crimes committed by Ishmael son of Nethaniah. Johanan and the officers fought against the rebels by

the great pool in Gibeon. ³⁴Ishmael escaped with eight of his men, but the remnant of Israel are rejoicing with Johanan for his victory. ³⁵They are following him to Egypt because they fear the Chaldeans, now that Gedaliah is dead. At this moment they are encamped near Bethlehem, and they are asking for you, Jeremiah! ³⁶'Has anyone seen our prophet Jeremiah?' they are asking. They want to seek your counsel. Will you come?"

## 43

In Bethlehem Jeremiah appeared small. He stood upon a stone step before the people, but he emitted no power. ²Beautiful man! How I love you! They long only for the fire in you, for your heart to whisk them as a fiery chariot to Heaven and back, with a cargo of answers . . . ³but I long for your gentle fingers and cool-water glances, the touch of you, the heart of flesh, the man of you.

⁴The people cried: "Grant our plea, and pray for us to the Lord your God , for all this remnant! ⁵For we remain but a few out of many, as you can see. ⁶Let the Lord *your* God tell us where we should go and what we should do."

⁷Jeremiah acquiesced. He said, "The Lord has not come to me since the capture of Jerusalem. ⁸But I will pray to the Lord who is not only *my* God but *your* God as well, as you request, and I will tell you whatever response the Lord gives for you. I will withhold nothing from you."

⁹Thereupon the people replied in unison: "Let the Lord be a true and faithful witness against us! ¹⁰We swear that we will do exactly as the Lord *your* God instructs us through you, whether pleasant or unpleasant!"

¹¹Jeremiah knelt upon the stone step and began to pray for response. He cradled his face in his hands. ¹²His body softly rocked and his tears flowed through his fingers, over his hands and down his arms, until his sleeves were soaked. ¹³He stayed this way for ten days. I watched him carefully during this time. ¹⁴I sat in the shadows and watched his rocking and supplicating. ¹⁵His tears, I could see, were spinning that God-shell around him, the way a caterpillar spins its cocoon. I had thought he had molted . . . ¹⁶I had thought he had pierced through that webbing and emerged a beautiful mortal man. But those tears and the words that he utters so lowly, so passionately, are spinning that God-shell, that impenetrable shell that makes him not man, but prophet . . . ¹⁷not mine, but His. These ten

days to me are the longest farewell. Farewell, Jeremiah. I shall ever wor-ship and adore you from afar ... [18]you the starry night and me the lone astrologer ... [19]but shall I ever hold you again? And shall you ever look my way? My husband, my life, farewell.

[20]At the end of ten days, Jeremiah assembled Johanan son of Kareah, all of the army officers, and all of the people, the remnant of Israel, great and small, and stood before them. [21]The sun struck my prophet and set him ablaze in a beacon of glowing amber light. The people leaned inward to hear, and my prophet spoke to them in thunderous tones:

[22]"Thus said the Lord, the God of Israel: If you remain in this land, I will build you and not overthrow, I will plant you and not uproot, for I regret the punishment I have brought upon you. [23]Do not be afraid of the king of Babylon, for I am with you to save you and to rescue you from his hands! [24]But if you say, 'No, we will go to the land of Egypt that we may not see war,' then hear the word of the Lord, O remnant of Judah! The sword that you fear shall overtake you there, and the famine you worry over shall follow at your heels, and there you shall die. [25]My wrath will be poured out upon you should you go to sojourn in Egypt. [26]And there shall be no surviving remnant of the disaster that I will bring upon you. Do not go to Egypt!"

[27]When Jeremiah had finished speaking all these words, the people responded "You are lying! The Lord *our* God did not send you to say, 'Don't go to Egypt.' [28]No! It is your scribe who is inciting you against us so that we may be killed by the Chaldeans or exiled to Babylon!"

[29]Baruch jolted at the sound of his name. The shock of what he heard struck him hard in the heart and he clutched his chest. [30]Jeremiah stood still as a pillar as the people turned away. Baruch dashed up to him. "Jeremiah! What have I done to be blasphemed like this!"

[31]Jeremiah responded, "It is me they blaspheme, Baruch. It is the prophet they persecute, not you. Never you. They could not care less about you. Only the prophet."

[32]"Are we to stay here, Jeremiah? Remain here, the only ones left in the land?"

[33]Jeremiah pondered this for a long moment. Then a strange sort of smile played upon his lips. [34]He said, "No, my friend. We will go with the people to Egypt."

[35]This was the day I saw the greatest change in my love, my prophet Jeremiah. He regained his power of prophecy, but it was forever changed by

the brief span he had spent with me in the gardens, in the quiet evenings wrapped in sheep-skin, touching and kissing my lips, my palms . . . [36]his brief rendezvous with normalcy made him defiant with God. [37]He was prepared, as never before, to disobey God's direct command to stay in the land, because he now tied his fate decidedly to the fate of the people. [38]All of his life, his soul, was in the hand of God. Now, he clasped his soul to his own self fiercely. [39]In this way, Jeremiah forever altered the nature of prophecy itself, for he made it clear to Heaven that the prophet is no puppet of God . . . that the prophet maintains a level of freedom to choose which direction to point his feet. [40]He would go with the people to Egypt, though God said clearly to him, 'Do not go to Egypt!' [41]He would go, and bind his fate with the remnant of Israel, if only to be among them . . . if only to ward off the terrible loneliness that had always been the life of any prophet.

# 44

And in this manner of righteous defiance, we arrived as strangers in the land of Egypt. [2]The first city we came upon was Tahpanhes, and the palace of the Pharaoh rose before us out of the land as monument to the artistry of man. [3]The painted brick formed a dazzling visual chant. [4]So these are the idols, O jealous God of Israel, with whom we are accused of whoring ourselves, these tall stone creatures with carved wings and vacant eyes. So these are those images that fill You with rage. [5]Ah, but God, they are inspiring tributes to the creativity of man . . . a creativity that You Yourself bestowed upon us, a gift You regret, that You long to extinguish. [6]Dear Lord, understand! that these are actually tributes to You, and Your magnificent creation of us . . . that You have enabled us to fill this world with beauty from stone, with magic from wind, why then does our appreciation of this gift fill You with such fear? [7]Why then do You long to stifle that which is so natural in man, so essential to man—the will to create? [8]Are You afraid these creations eclipse You? [9]On the contrary, my Lord and my Friend, I see the idols of Egypt and I am reminded of the majesty of the One God in heaven and earth. [10]You bring clay to life, Holy God, and we only mold it to resemble life.

[11]Jeremiah has assumed his place on the steps of the palace at Tahpanhes. [12]His mouth pours forth the Divine language and the remnant of Israel listens and argues. [13]They are fearless wrestlers of God like their

namesake Jacob. [14]I rest beneath a tree with a lapful of sweet wet dates. [15]I am a potter's studio, and the hand of God is in me, molding the clay. [16]He forms the tiny limbs and separates the fingers. He opens the eyelids a sliver and breathes gently into the nostrils. [17]Jeremiah fills the city with his ominous reports, and I sit contented, my belly filled with dates, my eyes closing drowsily, as I contemplate the turning and the pressing in my womb.

[18]All my life I have pursued ethereality to a point near absurdity. [19]But you, child, have jolted me into the world of the body. [20]You fastened yourself to me and plucked me out of a dream . . . into a world void of angels, but filled instead with a host of tiny physicalities: clumsiness, swollen capillaries, and aches. [21]All my life I have focused on the spiritual. Never on the physical. [22]But now, as I bend to turn the soil, you press against my pelvis. [23]You awakened me to muscles in my legs and ligaments of my abdomen. [24]My nasal passages, veins, navel, breasts, though always part of me, have never been as close as they are now. [25]They were far from my thoughts. [26]As you make yourself comfortable beneath my lungs, my 'breath of life' has become huffing, sighing, and panting.

[27]How tiny you must be, and yet you already cast your long shadow over all that is supernatural, and astonish me with the wonder of the natural. [28]While my body brings life to you, you bring to me, for the first time, anchorage.

[29]Thank you, child, for introducing me to the complexity and holiness of the outermost layer of this world. [30]Thank you for awakening me to the sensations of touch, taste, and smell. [31]Thank you for dimming my inner eye so that my two brown eyes could be flooded with colors. [32]Thank you for tuning me to the sounds of my self, rather than only that distant chiming of spirits and prophets. [33]Thank you for adding matter to form. Thank you for adding substance to dream. [34]Thank you for reminding me that soaring cedars have sturdy roots. [35]By making my body your dwelling-place, you have given my spirit a home, and the world has never seemed so intricate and replete.

[36]O mother Leah, first wife of Jacob! I understand now your love for your fourth child Judah! [37]With each son you bore, you thought, 'Ah, now my husband will love me, for I have born to him a son!' [38]But each time, Jacob's heart remained with Rachel. [39]So when you had your fourth child, and he lifted his round head and smiled to you, you thought not of your husband but only of your God. [40]You declared, "This time I will praise

God!" and the child became your son . . . not an offering to your husband to win his favor and love, but an offering to your own self, an angel of God fallen into your lap, entrusted to you, to be loved and cared after by you. [41] I can see that the bell of prophecy has fallen over my love. [42] I can see that he does not, cannot, turn to me, for the shield he now wears is binding. [43] I will not bring this child to him to barter for his affection, for it is futile. [44] Rather, I will bring this child into my heart, and love him as you loved Judah . . . this time I will praise God!

[45] Baruch draws near to me with a bucket filled with fish, onions, and leeks. [46] We bone the fish and chew on the savory bits even as Jeremiah promises the people that a sweeping famine will destroy us all. [47] I do not doubt the truth of his words. I only feel separate from them, as if I am watching a stage performance that I have seen many times before. [48] From the moment the fetters were released from us at Ramah, I have felt separate from the fate of the remnant of Israel. I have an independent fate, this much I know to be certain.

[49] "You are ripe, woman," Baruch said, "Your belly and breasts are full." [50] He wiped fish oil from his lips. "Look at us," he laughed. "Here we are, the scribe and the bride, devotedly trailing after an aging prophet. [51] O true, I know, Jeremiah's words are strong as youth. He bellows them out. But look at the way the people of Egypt regard him. [52] You know, they are polite, but in their eyes, they mock him. [53] He does not have the gold-jeweled staff or the gilded robes or the kingly sanction that their magicians bear. [54] As noble as he appears to us, my dear, and I do love him too, to the Egyptians he's a messy rapscallion. [55] You know, in the shadow of those detailed monuments—he seems small.

[56] "Well, this is it, my beauty. This is the land our forefathers escaped. This is the land of their oppression and their slavery. [57] Do you think any of those massive stones were carried by a bloodline of you or me?" [58] Baruch laughed to himself. "And we've come running back. [59] You know, Anatiya, it makes me wonder. They say that the land of Canaan was promised to us by God, you know? [60] And I, I just think we assume that when God promises us something it, well, it should be perfect. [61] But that is not the case. God promised us something that wasn't perfect . . . and you know, why not? [62] You point to the remnant of Israel gathered before us. I know what you mean. [63] God gave us an imperfect land so that we would make it perfect. Hmmm . . . and isn't it just the same with you and me—I mean,

with everyone? [64]This life, it isn't perfect. It isn't ever perfect. And yet, if we only made an effort, a little effort, we could dust it off and polish it up and turn it into a little bit of something divine. [65]Yes, I know what you mean. If everything were perfect there would be no room for us . . . no reason for us . . ."

[66]I wrote in the sand before us: Covenant.

[67]"Yes," Baruch said. "That's it. That's what I meant to say."

# 45

Under a date tree by the river Nile, a great tightening took hold of me as if the angel of death had seized me in an impassioned embrace. [2]I cried out in alarm and the remnant of Israel all turned their heads from their prophet to see. [3]Baruch cried out, "A midwife!" An Egyptian midwife and her daughter brought me to their tent. [4]The younger one mopped my brow with a sponge soaked in water and floral perfume. [5]The older one spoke foreign words over me and stroked my belly. [6]"Woe is me!" I heard the cry of my prophet as he addressed the remnant of Israel. [7]"The Lord has added grief to my pain. I am worn out with groaning, and I have found no rest!" [8]Everyone heard his cry as a lament for the people who would be plagued if they remained in Egypt, but only I knew those words as a double-edged sword, and for me, they cut to the core of my labor and pain. [9]O Eve! I do not curse you for this agony! [10]But I beg you, first woman and mother of all life, you who have witnessed every birth since the beginning, come to me! [11]Come Eve, and lead me wisely through!

[12]In the land of Egypt, among the remnant of Israel, in the humble, clean dwelling of a midwife and her daughter (a blessing upon their names!), [13]there was born to the prophet Jeremiah a son. [14]To the prophet Jeremiah and the woman who shadowed him all of his days like a faint aroma of meadow, like a distant memory of lilies abloom in the valley of Sharon, a child-spook, a brittle tea leaf, a muted prophetess, Anatiya, was born a son.

# 46

The word of the Lord came to the prophet Jeremiah that he had begot a son. <sup>2</sup>"Concerning your son, Jeremiah," said Baruch. "What shall he be called?"

<sup>3</sup>Jeremiah replied, "Let his name not be linked with mine, lest he suffer the same trials and anguish. <sup>4</sup>Let him not be the son of a prophet, that he not be charged with a mission as mine, that he not be accused and mistreated, <sup>5</sup>that God not command me to take him to the mountaintop, that he not fear as did I all his life . . . <sup>6</sup>not out of the ways of a man and a woman was he made, but from my seed spilled into a warm bath. <sup>7</sup>Let him therefore be called Ben Zera, son of seed."

<sup>8</sup>O child!
Sweetest package in my arms,
the scent of a garden that God has kissed
clings to you. <sup>9</sup>I breathe you
and a wave of pleasure rushes over me
as though I had never known air
until it was filled with the petals of your perfume,
<sup>10</sup>as though I had never known sky
until it reflected the soft pastels shed from your cheeks.
<sup>11</sup>Your head is a ripe melon, soft as the fruit of a melon.
<sup>12</sup>You are crowned with brown curls
that some artful angel embroidered with gold thread.
<sup>13</sup>Your hair is soft as the finest sand
where no foot has tread.
<sup>14</sup>Your eyes are the dark blue of the sky before dawn
streaked with black rays.
<sup>15</sup>Your nose is just a pinch of pink clay . . .
What Artist has made you?
<sup>16</sup>Whose brushstroke did color you?
None other than our Creator,
the Lord my God,
to Whom I shall lift you up
in praise and adoration

~WROTE ANATIYA.

[17]The parting of your lips is the parting of the Jordan
that Joshua and his men did cross, to
enter the promised land.
[18]Enter my breast.
[19]I shall flow like the land with milk and with honey.
[20]If never you wean,
never will I mumble for release . . .
but I will follow you as Miriam's well did follow the wanderers,
[21]that you may lower your mouth to my waters
as a gazelle lowers his mouth to a stream.
[22]And I will quietly sparkle before you . . .
and if I should dry up while feeding your thirst,
so let me dry up.
[23]It would be the sweetest death.

[24]You clench your toes and your fingers as you suckle.
[25]You murmur a syrupy sort of song
which the birds cock their head and study.
[26]'Amen, amen,'
my heart says to you,
your limbs are a plump bouquet in my arms.
[27]'Amen, amen,'
my heart sings to your Creator,
for such detailed and delicate design.
[28]This babe will worship You, Lord.
This babe will walk in the paths of the righteous.

[29]I love you.

[30]Chariots dash madly
and horses advance,
warriors go forth,
they grasp the shield
and draw the bow.
[31]Yet I cannot elicit a single tear, my son,
for the healing you have brought me

is utterly complete.
³²My eyes shall not be red from weeping.
And though the plagues persist,
and the wrath of the Lord charges on comets,
the remedy of you is so thorough, my love.
³³I cannot falter,
I cannot fear,
for you are with me.

³⁴The word of the Lord comes to Jeremiah about the coming of King Nebuchadrezzar of Babylon to attack the land of Egypt.

³⁵He stands there, your father,
wrapped in his rainbow,
with colors streaming from his mouth.
³⁶Colors of blood and silver sword.
³⁷The people tremble before him.
³⁸The Egyptians begin to take heed.
³⁹His body is wracked with lightning
that none other can see.
⁴⁰I hold you in my arms and stand
amidst the people,
only I standing firm,
only I unafraid.
⁴¹He does not look to you, my child,
but know assuredly that he feels you,
he dreams you,
and he longs to look,
but the grip of prophecy denies him.

⁴²Zipporah's husband, Moses, knew the grip of prophecy well, and he could not descend to his family. ⁴³And so, Zipporah herself raised the flint to her son and circumcised his flesh, as the Lord of Hosts commands. ⁴⁴By the river Nile I lay you, my son, and unwrap the swaddling cloth. ⁴⁵Baruch, my friend, does hold your legs. Your arms are flung wide to embrace all of Heaven, and you raise your voice to make yourself known. ⁴⁶I wield the knife swiftly and you shed a drop of blood. The holiest offering. ⁴⁷Life, God's promise, like the land, is not perfect, but through our role in

the covenant we raise it up to the heights. [48]"This is what I meant to say," says Baruch. "We make it so. That we must make it so."

[49]I wash you and swaddle you in a white linen cloth.
[50]Come to me, my love,
I tell you,
no other blade shall touch you,
no other sword shall cut,
for you have given of your flesh and your blood
as a ransom for your life
that you may hereafter live
in blessing.
[51]The years rolling out before you
are satiated with dew,
and your body and breath
are rooted in God.

[52]Little lamb, little lamb,
none shall harm you,
and your Shepherd will count you
among His flock

~WROTE ANATIYA.

[53]Your father recites at the Lord's dictation:
"I will make an end of all nations
among which I have banished you."
[54]You may wonder someday
why the nations are punished,
for though they plundered and razed our people, our land,
they only served as God's tool against Israel.
[55]Could they and should they have resisted God's will?
These are questions, my love, that I cannot answer,
but perhaps in your day
you will lead us to discern
and to know before Whom we stand.

## 47

Thus wrote Anatiya:

Angels! bring Jeremiah tidings.
²You will find him locked high in a tower,
a tower that scrapes at the firmament.
³Angels! rush Jeremiah news.
You will find him high in a tower
surrounded by a moat wide as the sky
that no man can cross.
⁴But you may reach him, Godspeed,
and announce these words to him . . .
that his son has his almond eyes,
that his son has his swath of silk hair,
⁵that I hear his son laugh
and it sounds a wind chime,
⁶that his touch is the touch of butterfly wings
and roses are pressed into his cheeks.
⁷Be swift! and tell him
that the child is wise,
for he knows how to suckle
and how to relieve,
and what more need a man to know?
⁸Angels! do tell him
that the child is strong,
that he reaches for the moon-sliver,
grasps its beautiful beams
and does not let them slip.
⁹Tell him! that the child has healed well
and his speech is the speech that all creatures spoke
before language was scrambled at the tower of Babel.
¹⁰His words none can comprehend,
but they inspire and capture the hearts of all.
¹¹With his two or three syllables,
he is a master orator.

¹²Tell my prophet! that though he is tormented
with visions of the end,
his son knows only beginning.
His son knows only serenity.
¹³All should learn
and all should see,
the child is good.
The child is very good.
¹⁴Go, angels! Go!

¹⁵The angels replied to me:
"The prophet is already aware of this."
So you see, my child,
he knows.
He already knows.

## 48

O child,
if God were a woman
would the land be laid waste?
Would the towns all be ravaged?
²Would She act the jealous spouse
and punish Israel's roaming?
³If God were a woman
would She be as needy of our praise,
would She want a House of high limestone walls
and a daily portion of sheep and goats
slaughtered at the neck
and laid on the fire?
⁴Would She find the smell
of roasting meat pleasant?
⁵If God were a woman
would Her wrath be all-consuming?
⁶Would She urge the nations to war

and lead them into battle?
[7]Would She barrel over brides and babies
and the young men full of confidence and passion,
would She reap with Her scythe
the old men and old women,
though their mistakes may have been many,
would She not forgive them?
[8]With their bones brittle
and faces creased and sun-bronzed,
with their hearts innocently elated
at the fresh aroma of a clean sheet
hung on the line, or the rub and purr
of a hungry street kitten?
[9]If God were a woman
would She think us sinners,
or simply strayed sheep
who need rounding up,
who are instinctively, blamelessly lured
by the glimmer of green pastures
over yonder way?
[10]If God were a woman
would She condemn our faults,
or would She coddle and console us
in our many shortcomings?
[11]Would She threaten us with terror
and dangle over us the sword,
and withhold Heaven's rains
so that the earth cracks and dries
and screams from heat,
[12]would She think our unworthiness
punishable by death?
[13]If God were a woman
would She choose one over the other
and incite brother against brother,
would She shower fire and brimstone upon us?

[14]If God were a woman
would She pummel us with rules
and command us to obey,
while implanting within us the impulse
to step out of the bounds
and explore wild territories outside the Garden?
[15]Would She use the prophets as Her messengers
to bark and snarl at us through their mouths,
or would She speak to each one directly,
in gentler tones,
or would She speak at all with words,
or rather, would She speak through thought and dream,
through the dance of the trees
and the shades of the sun in its stages,
through tea leaves and migration patterns
and the slow spiral of shells
and flowers unfurling?
[16]If God were a woman
would She judge us by the same standards
as the angels,
who are all gold and no dross,
all breath and no clay,
would She deny the power of the earth in us
that leads us to lust and directs us in wanton ways,
would She dispute the carnal element in our creation
and condemn us for what we struggle to control?
[17]If God were a woman
would She hide her face from us
to have us search our whole lives in vain?
Would Her love be conditional?
[18]If God were a woman
would She oppose the great truth: that mortality fills a person with
    fear,
and that fear drives a person to think madly?
That a person toils to silence that dread

with bigger and faster and louder living?

¹⁹Know, child,
that God transcends both woman and man,
compassion and judgment,
understanding and strength.
²⁰Only at times, the woman-side is concealed.
²¹At times,
like the mother-bird,
She is shooed from the nest.
And we, the eggs,
remain

~WROTE ANATIYA.

²²Jeremiah is counting out the nations, numbering the cities that are sure to be crushed. ²³You must know, my love, that it was Cain who created the first city in the world. ²⁴Cain, who murdered his brother in a fit of jealousy, was banished from the land. The farm no longer yielded to his touch. ²⁵And so he wandered and settled in the land of Nod, east of Eden. ²⁶There he built the first city, which he named for his son Enoch. ²⁷And so, my son, a city is a place that has, inherent in its very design, memory of the first violence, because its founder was the first murderer. ²⁸Every city is a manifestation of the ego of Cain. When you walk in a city, you can sense a stalking, sense a low-grade anger crouched beneath the heat, sense that your neighbor is unsatisfied with his lot. ²⁹Better, my son, for you to return to your father's land in Anatot. There you shall lay me to rest.

³⁰Do you see, child?
The way the horizon is hazy and blurred?
And how the land dips down and disappears?
³¹The sages of old taught that the world is round.
They watch the curve of the clouds and know.
³²The Egyptians watch the stars astutely
and see they travel in cycles.
³³The Babylonians know of a polar star

that returns every 36,000 years.
You see? [34]There is great wisdom in every culture
and great beauty in their art.
[35]You will hear them say that the Moabites and Ammonites
are descendents of incest between a father and his daughters.
[36]You will hear them say the Philistines are vulgar and crude.
[37]You will hear them say that the Edomites eat their animals alive.
[38]You will hear such things about other nations,
and to be sure, they too spread falsehoods about us,
[39]but I tell you, son,
every culture has its own great wisdom.
Every culture owns a fragment of the map
that leads to truth,
that leads to good.


[40]Are we the chosen people, you will wonder?
[41]Yes, we are chosen . . .
chosen to be us.
And they are chosen to be they,
and each is chosen for a purpose under Heaven.
[42]You must understand this:
As sure as I am chosen,
I am also, as certainly, not chosen.
[43]I am chosen to be me,
and at the same time,
I am chosen not to be anyone else.
[44]Just the same are you chosen and not chosen . . .
chosen to be you
and not chosen to be anyone other than you.
[45]Every culture has its pride
as every culture has its shame . . .
but know this, my child, and take it to heart:


[46]Love people, and you shall love God.
Love people, and you shall love God.

⁴⁷Know this.
You will hear that all idolaters are fools,
but even our God Who rules heaven and earth,
even our God (forgive me!) can Himself become an idol,
⁴⁸if you allow your worship of Him
to come between you and treating your neighbors with kindness.
⁴⁹More than sacrifice and more than song,
more than feast and festivity,
⁵⁰God wants you to welcome the stranger,
comfort the bereaved,
clothe the naked,
invite the lonely,
embolden the weak,
seek peace and pursue justice
in every corner . . .
⁵¹for all people and God are inexorably linked.
⁵²Love people, therefore, and you shall love God

~WROTE ANATIYA.


⁵³Do you see, child?
Egypt is an extraordinary place.
⁵⁴Take its majesty into your heart as did Joseph,
as did Moses,
but remember, no matter the wonders you encounter,
remember who you are
and be true to your heritage.
⁵⁵For you can travel the world and see every great sight
and study every great writ,
and in the end you will have a mish-mash philosophy
quilted shabbily together.
⁵⁶Rather, look with your eyes,
listen with your ears, and appreciate all . . .
but devote your heart solely
to your own inheritance,

for then your identity will be solid and true,
the road before you clearly marked,
and this journey will take you farther and deeper
than skimming the surface of every interesting thing.
⁵⁷This journey will unlock the resources
that lie in deep recesses of your soul.
⁵⁸Believe me, my love, when I tell you,
venturing out and exploring becomes tiresome and boring
over time. ⁵⁹Rather, settle in, when you are ready,
with a bride and a home,
make your study a routine,
and you will find every dawn a new day
with surprises and sweetness at every turn

~WROTE ANATIYA.

## 49

Thus wrote Anatiya:

I remember Jeremiah in his youth.
²His body was wispy as a branch
with a willowy length of hair.
³Long before Baruch the scribe,
I was there beside him.
⁴Long before God created the world
He frolicked with His companion
and Her name was Wisdom.
⁵He created the world with Wisdom.
⁶He created the world in Wisdom,
for She was His constant delight.

⁷I am the heart of the prophet.
Though he consulted me not with words,
though he turned not his head to me,
he drew strength from my attendance,

he sapped me at times of my life force.
[8]I was his vigor. I was his heart.

[9]And the prophet created a world with me.
[10]The prophet created a world in me.
[11]I was Jeremiah's companion
just as Wisdom accompanied God.
[12]I am the twin-soul of the prophet
that was never entirely severed.

[13]Assuredly, the day is coming
when my life shall be no more,
when I shall be gathered to my kin
and return, amidst choirs, to the Source of all Life.
[14]On that day,
the prophecies of Jeremiah will cease

~WROTE ANATIYA.

[15]Bring me a scroll, Baruch,
quills and a bottle of ink.
[16]I shall gather all these scraps.
[17]I shall arrange all these notes I have taken
from the beginning
and record them in a scroll
as a testament of my life
and a chronicle on how it is
to love a prophet.

[18]Open the scroll before me.
It is wide and blank
and it stretches like the desert before the slaves.
[19]How to take the first step?
How to make the first mark?
How to sully the blank page
and touch pen to parchment?

²⁰How to take a private life
and report it in permanence
when language can only one angle perceive?

²¹I shall start:
The words of Anatiya, daughter of Avigayil, one of the handmaids at the
temple at Anatot in the territory of Benjamin.

²²My body is not so smooth and so taut
as in my youth.
²³My hair is not so lustrous,
its color is drained and peppered gray.
²⁴My gait is not so lively
and my passion not so keen.
²⁵This body of earth shall return to earth,
this body of water will nourish a field,
this body of air will reunite with sky.
²⁶The fire of me will quicken in you,
and you will bear my torch,
and reinterpret its flames
for yourself.

²⁷I need, my love, to return to Anatot.
²⁸I need the familiar glint of wheat in the sun.
²⁹I need the heap of stones that once was the well
where we watered the flock.
It is time to return home.

³⁰Lo, Jeremiah is gleaming still.
³¹His hair is a cloud of ice crystals
evaporating in cool mist in the sun.
³²I love him, how my heart runs to him,
but I have not the strength any longer
to contend with the Almighty.
³³Rather, I have locked my love eternally

in the deepest chamber of my heart,
the most sacred shrine,
and my blood beats through him.
³⁴But I have opened other chambers
that had hitherto been vaulted . . .
and God, my archrival,
has streamed softly in . . .
³⁵God of withered leaves and wilted flowers,
God of seasons changing
and surf withdrawing . . .
³⁶He has come to walk me home,
to hold my hand
and be my Companion.

³⁷Come, my child,
and I shall take you to my home,
though I know you have love for the Nile.
³⁸You trudge through her muddy banks
smiling in the fertile slop.
³⁹You scoop up pebbles and rocks
and snatch at fishes that are too fast for you.
⁴⁰Young boy, but another river courses through your heart,
and her name is the Jabbok . . .
the river beside which our patriarch Jacob did wrestle.
⁴¹There you will wrestle,
and there you will thrive,
for a flower grows hearty
when watered at the roots
in native soil.

⁴²Before we depart I shall make known our intent to Baruch

~WROTE ANATIYA.

⁴³"Baruch," I wrote, "my only friend. I am returning with Ben Zera to Anatot." ⁴⁴Baruch studied the note and then lifted his eyes. "O, Anatiya," he sighed and took up my hands. ⁴⁵"I will say good-bye only when you are

breathing your last." ⁴⁶In this way he chose to accompany us back to the land. ⁴⁷We gathered provisions all the next day and loaded them onto the asses. ⁴⁸People observed and inquired, and Baruch said we were returning to the land. ⁴⁹One family, then another, and then one more, decided without persuasion to join our small caravan, and thus a portion of the remnant returned.

⁵⁰I look to my prophet. He stands on the steps.
⁵¹Shall I see you again? I wonder.
⁵²And does it matter?—
for your image is embedded in my heart
and scorched into my eyes.
You are always before me.
⁵³"I love you!"
I stand on my tiptoes
to see above the crowd
and I call to him
with blaring heart,
though silent lips.
⁵⁴In the midst of his prophecy he answered my cry,
saying "How the glorious city is deserted,
the citadel of my joy!"
⁵⁵I blinked tears for the prophet
and withdrew from the place.
⁵⁶I will not spend four hundred years here in Egypt.
⁵⁷I will not spend forty years finding my home.
⁵⁸I shall leave now and directly,
though my love stays behind.
⁵⁹You must understand, Jeremiah,
I cannot die here
to be wrapped in rags and encased in a tomb.
⁶⁰I will die in Anatot,
and dissolve
and become the very land I love ...
and my son shall visit me there
and his children's children will make pilgrimage.

⁶¹Until Eden, my love,
until then,
when I see you again
amidst wildflower and fruit,
until Eden,
I bid you farewell.

### 50

The journey to Anatot is long
and the desert rises and falls around us
in undulating hues of gold.
²In the afternoons the families gather
in the shade of pitched tents
around kettles of sweetened tea.
³Nobody murmurs about the journey.
Nobody longs to turn back.
The land is calling us each to return.
⁴She is a long lost love
whom we thought had rejected us,
but sends us a sudden sign
that the heart is healed.
⁵We run to relieve her loneliness.

⁶O Zion!
Time has raked over your settlements
and uprooted your grasses.
⁷Your pastures are parched
and your righteous are searching for shade.
⁸Your children have hungry circles 'round their eyes,
and your cisterns are filled with dead.
⁹Even so!
The naked beauty of you grips me.
Your bared breast takes hold of me.
¹⁰And though your stones glint

with the memory of flashes of metal,
and though your children
reap in tears
and sow in blood,
[11]your loveliness is never compromised.
[12]Stripped of your ornaments
and made swarthy by the sun,
you remain my soul's delight,
and you beckon me.
[13]Your beauty beckons me,
I shall rebuild you.

[14]In the day that I returned to Anatot

~WROTE ANATIYA

my whole body felt serene.
[15]Every muscle that had been tightened and wound
since the days of my youth
were released and were calmed
and my heart felt at ease.
[16]Here is where the circle began.
Here is where the circle will end.
[17]I see the beginning of the circle
here in the end,
and it brings me the softest comfort.

[18]Baruch pitched a tent and Ben Zera followed him
close on his heals, wherever he went.
[19]I lay out a sheet of parchment
and a fan of new quills.
[20]I could feel the land desire to speak through me.
I could feel God in my heart start to whisper.
[21]I wrote:

Thus speaks the land:
Children, come home!
Nest in me, be near,
the cold moon rustles
my untamed fields.
<sup>22</sup>My lakes are frigid and forlorn
even in the torrid sun.
<sup>23</sup>Forget me not, children!
I shall help you to remember.
I shall deposit myself, grain by grain,
into your eyes at night.
<sup>24</sup>When you yawn and you rub them,
you will conjure me up
behind your sleepy lids.
<sup>25</sup>I shall call to you in the night
in your dreams.

<sup>26</sup>A man approached me timorously.
He inquired softly, "May I look?"
<sup>27</sup>He had the manner of a mouse
that might dart away if frightened at all.
<sup>28</sup>I nodded and the man drew near the parchment.
<sup>29</sup>He read the words I had written
and he burst into tears.
<sup>30</sup>"Please, author, may I read more?"
<sup>31</sup>The man leafed through the pages of parchment
that had yet to be sewn into a scroll.
<sup>32</sup>"This!" he exclaimed, holding one up,
"May I sing this? May I put this to music?"
<sup>33</sup>And he drew out a reed-flute
and while looking at the words
the man began to play a melody with long, doleful notes,
and sorrowful sounds.
<sup>34</sup>He lowered the flute from his mouth
and sang my words in the same melody.

<sup>35</sup>He switched from the words to the reed and back
until the song was familiar and he sang with great confidence.
<sup>36</sup>As his voice carried,
another man appeared from just over the hill,
and a family from a meadow not far beyond that.
<sup>37</sup>Soon there were forty or so people who had joined
to hear the new song, to learn it and sing.
<sup>38</sup>They drew out their drums, lutes, lyres, and trumpets
and lifted their voices until the song became a celebration.
<sup>39</sup>The man who had been so timid at first said to me,
"Here you see the true remnant of Israel and Judah.
<sup>40</sup>We never joined the band that left for Egypt.
We stayed in the land and coordinated our strengths,
so that the food that we harvest we share between all.
<sup>41</sup>We lay low and keep hidden,
and the Chaldeans in general just let us be.
<sup>42</sup>You see? We are the true remnant of Israel and Judah,
and we are very few.
But we are very proud.
<sup>43</sup>We are the stragglers who have been faithful all along.
<sup>44</sup>Won't you be our poet and inspiration?
Won't you prophesy for us?
<sup>45</sup>For Jeremiah left for Egypt with the people,
and we have been surviving in quiet ever since."

<sup>46</sup>Won't I prophesy?
But do you not see?
I am no prophet.
I am merely the heart of a prophet.

<sup>47</sup>"Her name is Anatiya,
but the prophet Jeremiah called her Jerusalem,"
I turned and saw Baruch speaking to the people.
<sup>48</sup>I hid my face for I felt exposed and flushed,
though a thrill ran through my fingertips . . .

an urge to write verses for this true remnant.
⁴⁹"She cannot speak,
but she will write her words in this scroll
every day by this tree.
⁵⁰And if you need solace,
and if you need soothing,
sit beside her as she writes,
read her words as her quill spills them,
for in them and between them, you shall find your relief."

⁵¹Day after day,
they gather beside me under the date tree.
⁵²Sometimes it is few, and other times there are many.
⁵³Sometimes it is just children who sit with their hands folded
and study the letters. ⁵⁴Other times it is the elderly who come
and watch with wise eyes.
⁵⁵The verses I write become the song the people sing as they work.
⁵⁶The people are bolstered and their cheeks become rosy.
⁵⁷They rest with me,
shovel or spade in their hand,
or they spread out their evening meal as I work,
and their goodness does fill me.
⁵⁸I long to carve out my soul for them
and present it to them in gilded letters,
for these are the loyal children of the land.
⁵⁹The land loves them
and little by little,
she yields to them
and they celebrate her seasons with joy.

⁶⁰There are times
when I fall into a trance,
when I feel myself far away,
lingering over the date tree.
⁶¹I look down at myself as I write in the scroll.

$^{62}$I look down at the people who nibble baskets
of berries and nuts.
$^{63}$And I lay upon the air
and float as on water
with no fear of falling.
$^{64}$And when I return and my eyes are my own,
the words I have written are not.
$^{65}$They are lyrics from some other place,
from some other hand,
but I dare not discard them.
$^{66}$Is this how it was for you, Jeremiah?
Are you sometimes somewhere
above the Temple step where you preach?
$^{67}$And in this place, are you peaceful
and solitary, and the bruising and jeering
is nothing at all?
$^{68}$If this is so,
then why does the prophet cry?

$^{69}$Remnant of Israel and Judah,
your callused hands are more gentle than a baby's touch.
$^{70}$The bread that you bake remains fresh, never stale,
and it is filled with hints of honey.
$^{71}$Your sheep and your goats are strong and robust
and they never roam far from your staff.
$^{72}$Their milk is a thick and sweet cream.
$^{73}$Remnant of Israel and Judah,
pomegranate juice runs down your chin
and rich olive oil flows through your beard.
$^{74}$Your figs are plump and your grapes hang down
in ripe luscious tendrils. $^{75}$You are lovely,
you are lovely, the gold of the land
has been soaked into your skins,
every man of you is Adam
and every woman of you is Eve,

and no tree in the middle of the garden can tempt you.
⁷⁶You are content with the gracious offerings of the Lord.
And God is content to live among you.

⁷⁷The iniquity of Israel shall be sought,
and there shall be none.
⁷⁸The sins of Judah,
and none shall be found.
For I will pardon those I allow to survive.

⁷⁹My son shall be among you
and he shall study all your ways.
⁸⁰Though he never heard me speak,
he shall hear his mother's voice
in your songs . . .
in the words you put to music.

## 51

Thus wrote Anatiya:

On the day that I die
my life will flash before me eyes
²and though it will be in the space of a moment
I will watch as if it were the longest production.
³Indeed, I will be wrapped in the scroll of my life
like a caterpillar in a cocoon, and my whole body
will soak up the images of my life. ⁴At the end of the scroll
there will be a long stairway,
like the ladder in Jacob's night vision,
like the steps of the high ziggurat.
⁵I will cry, as any thoughtful reader cries at the end,
and my spirit will caress my cheek
and kiss away my tears until I am exhausted
and fall asleep.

[6]Then, my little soul will poke and nip through the scroll.
[7]It will shake itself loose and blink in the Godlight.
[8]It will undoubtedly be damp and a little sticky,
and so it will take some time to dry on the grass.
[9]Then, it will take a deep breath,
so deep, deeper than the breath of a sail on a giant ship,
and it will fly like a moth to the moon.
[10]It will sail into the sea,
the upper sea,
which has fathomless depths but is thinner than a thread.
[11]Too thin for me to fathom.
It will sail out to this sea
like a heavy fog,
and rain crystal tears into the waters
and add to this sea my memories.

[12]My son,
it is often that we love the ones
who are not with us even more than the ones who are . . .
even more than we love ourselves.
[13]After I die, my love,
while you are yearning for me,
you must remember that I am yearning for you as well . . .
[14]not to join me soon, for that day will come,
but rather for you to live a life
full of loving and learning,
doing and being.
[15]It is important to remember
that the dead never vanish.
[16]They continue to support the world
and nudge and coax its inhabitants,
with downy little touches,
to live fully.

[17]And so,
if you should forget my face someday,
if you should forget the feel of my embrace,
do not cry.
Do not stomp.
[18]For know this, my love,
when your memory of me begins to fade,
it is me who is choosing to withdraw some memories,
like the sea draws in the surf at low tide
in order to provide the shore some relief,
in order to make room for new memories.
[19]It is out of love.

[20]I have spent my life caught in the orbit of a prophet.
[21]My passion ignited me for him,
and my breath did burn like the flames of Leviathan.
[22]I dwelt in shadows and nooks
like a dove in the cranny of the rock,
and I spied upon him day and night.
[23]At times my love so overpowered,
I unabashedly wanted to steal him from God,
to pluck him from Israel to keep as my own.
[24]I have learned now
that there was always a plan
and that Heaven is good.
[25]Dear God, how You tolerated the antics of a child!
[26]I romped in the woods
and roamed in the Temple.
[27]I exposed my nakedness to trees
and scattered Your holy altar's fire.
[28]And yet, You did not count me among the unfaithful.
You have sustained me until this day.

<sup>29</sup>I never loved another than Jeremiah
and no other man knew me.
I could not run from him.
I could not flee.

<sup>30</sup>I saw the downfall of Israel and Zion.
I sat in the gate while Jeremiah was in jail.
<sup>31</sup>I was there when the walls of the city were breached.
<sup>32</sup>I held the orphans of the city close to my breast.
<sup>33</sup>I laid the soldiers to rest and consoled the bereaved.
<sup>34</sup>I was among the captured exiled to Babylon,
fettered and hungry.
<sup>35</sup>I was released to remain in the land with Gedaliah.
<sup>36</sup>There my prophet lay in my arms.
<sup>37</sup>Those were the happiest times,
though the land was laid waste,
though the people in chains,
we lived as if on an island,
without fear or dread,
and thought the worst had passed.
<sup>38</sup>And then, I witnessed Gedaliah's murder
and the slaughter of many more.
<sup>39</sup>Their bodies dropped before me as I hid.
The sky was raining corpses.
The clouds were splattered with blood.
<sup>40</sup>We joined the people in caravan to Egypt.
We undid the Exodus of our people
and returned to the land of our oppression,
although it was not oppressive.
<sup>41</sup>We encamped by the Nile and dined
on buckets of fish.
<sup>42</sup>There, you were born,
with the aid of two Egyptian midwives
with kind voices and easy massage.
<sup>43</sup>In my eyes you eclipsed

every terror in this world,
and even, a little,
the radiant rays
that emanated from my prophet.
⁴⁴I knew I had to bring you home to Anatot.
⁴⁵Here, I have seen the true remnant of Israel and Judah.
⁴⁶They are a righteous, God-fearing people
whom the angels and Heaven do love.

⁴⁷At death we are inhaled back into the Source.
It is a return trip.
Death is a coming home . . .
⁴⁸to the familiar smell of wool and wheat,
bread baking, oil frying . . .
⁴⁹Here, God says, have a seat.
The fire is warm and the light flickers against the walls.
⁵⁰I will warm my hands
and my eyes will become heavy.
⁵¹My mind will drift.
I will close them . . .
if only for the briefest moment . . .
for a rest,
⁵²the kind of rest you can only have at home.
⁵³When I open my eyes, the dwelling has vanished,
the fire is gone,
the tea is empty,
but God is everywhere and

I am

~WROTE ANATIYA.

[54]There are things that I need you to remember,
things I have learned:
[55]A tree that is nourished by a hidden source,
a concealed fountain,
is like a city that has deeply hewn cisterns.
[56]Without these, the city could not survive
under a long, drawn-out siege.

[57]A tree that is nourished by a hidden source,
a concealed fountain,
is like a person with a deep imagination.
[58]Without this, the person could not survive
alienation, ridicule, or sorrow.

[59]What is the difference between a fountain and a well?
[60]A well reaches down into the belly of the earth
the way breath reaches down into the breast.
[61]We access the sweet waters ourselves,
lowering a pail and lifting it again with our strength.
[62]A well demands that we participate
in the fulfillment of its task.

[63]A fountain generates its own energy,
reaching into the earth and into the sky at the same time.
[64]Its waters are constantly churning and refreshing themselves.
One need only to offer one's lips and the waters leap up to kiss them.

[65]Are you a fountain or a well?
[66]Do you need others to bring you out,
or do you inspire yourself from within?

[67]A tree that is nourished by a hidden source,
a concealed fountain,
is like a heart with deep faith.

[68]Without this, the heart could not endure
seeing its effort for good
being swallowed by the advocates of hate.

[69]A locked fountain is the earth's virginity.
[70]The fountain hides, and so it takes no praise for itself.
[71]However, its beauty is deceived by the roots it feeds,
by the blush of the petals
and the perfume of lilac and roses,
for the joy of flowers is never quiet.
[72]They sing with color and bat their frilly lashes
around wide smiling eyes.

[73]There is one fountain that nourishes all,
and this fountain is called love.
[74]Just as a fountain never runs dry
no matter how many buckets are filled,
so too does love regenerate itself,
ever-flowing, spilling from one heart to another.
[75]The waters of this hidden fountain are love,
and its garden is lush with passion-fruit.
[76]Love itself cannot be seen,
but its effects on the ones who feels themselves loved
are bountiful.

[77]Take a vessel of water.
Tilt it in many directions,
without letting a drop spill.
[78]Notice that the water always remains level
no matter the position of the glass.

[79]So too with unconditional love:
no matter the crookedness of the vessel,
love sees the soul inside is pure,
and love remains unchanged,
steady and true

~WROTE ANATIYA.

[80]Some think, my son, that the stars have a power of their own.
Let the stars then save them.
[81]Some think that money has the power of a deity.
Let that wealth stand up and save them.
[82]Some think that they have the power to save themselves.
It is very lonely at the top.
[83]We are not under our own authority.
We exist under Authority from above,
as do the stars.
[84]What does this mean?
This means that just as the stars
are commanded in their course,
so are we commanded in ours.
[85]Commanded! And what is our course?
[86]To give to the poor.
[87]To feed the hungry.
[88]To mend clothing for the naked.
[89]To treat our neighbor with kindness and respect,
[90]not so that we should feel good about ourselves,
but because we are commanded,
as a soldier is commanded.

[91]We are commanded to love.
[92]We are not commanded to befriend,
only to love.
[93]See a fragment of Divine light in every face,
in every pair of eyes.
[94]Whether you like the vessel or not, this is not the concern.
[95]Only love the light that shines from within the vessel.
[96]Love the light and cherish it
in every mysterious other

~WROTE ANATIYA.

[97]Pursue wisdom, my child,
but know first of all
that this is no skip through the pasture.
[98]This is a tiresome mountain climb
and the summit is far beyond your years,
but there are treasures along the way.

[99]The pursuit of wisdom is tiresome and hard.
[100]But when we choose not to know,
when we opt not to learn,
when we say no to wisdom, we say no to rain.

[101]When we say no to wisdom,
we allow an entire region of ourselves to dry up
and we allow for a hollowing of the soul.
[102]Ignorance is blight.
[103]A desert creeps in and settles and spreads,
swallowing our soil-rich fruited plains
until we feel a widening blankness—
[104]not a creative blankness
like that of the pristine blank page,
but a feverish chalk-choked blankness
that needs and needs, but will not receive.
[105]It mourns its own hunger,
and laments its own void.
[106]The soul is easily lost in this place.

[107]When we choose not to gain knowledge,
we deny creation to whole regions of ourselves.
[108]We throw a ratty mat over a flowerbed and watch it die
while we sit on top and chew on crusts of bread.

[109]There is nothing so perfect
as a wall with a door and a window.
[110]A wall to shelter,

a door to invite in,
to leave through and come back through,
to close and to open to the vast space,
and a window through which to know truth

~WROTE ANATIYA.

[111]I am tired.
I shall soon lay down my quill.
[112]Go forth, my child,
and learn.
[113]Learn, my child,
and teach,
for I can teach you no more.
[114]The sparrow rests on the eagle's back
and when the eagle, from fatigue, can carry her no more,
the rested sparrow jumps up and flies even higher.
[115]Fly even higher, my child,
even higher than I.
[116]I am tired.
I have had a lovely swim
in a large, freshwater fountain,
long gulps of clean water,
and now I shall dive down to the depths,
and now I shall burst up to the heights.
[117]I am tired, my child.
Come curl in my lap.
[118]My handwriting is slow
and the letters are dropping
and slanting downward
toward the corner of the page.
[119]I find my thought,
my thought is somewhere else,
[120]I have wearied myself for fire,
I have wearied myself for fire,
[121]now comes the quenching,

billowing wing,

sailing on waters,

my last image,

the sapphire pavement,

the ocean, its laughing froth,

let me only,

let me only say

I

[122]Thus far the words of Anatiya. I, Baruch son of Neriah, did compile this scroll from the writings of Anatiya daughter of Avigayil. [121]The prophet Jeremiah did return in the days before her death. [122]Soon after her leaving Egypt, his prophesying had ended. [123]For three days the prophet did hold his bride in his arms, and when she died he kissed her eyelids closed. [124]Jeremiah did wrap Anatiya in his own garment and carried her body into her grave. [125]He lay her down gently and with love, and filled the grave with soft earth with his own hands. [126]The prophet Jeremiah did instruct me to bury him beside his bride in the day of his death, and I did promise him this. [127]Anatiya was gathered to her kin and buried in Anatot.

## 52

The name my father, the prophet Jeremiah, gave me was Ben Zera, which was the source of much teasing for me as a youth. [2]I changed the name to Ben Sira, the letters of which have the same numerical value as the name Jeremiah. [3]I was raised by the good and kindly scribe Baruch, who educated me in his fine art, and we lived among the true remnant of Israel and Judah. [4]I left to follow the journey of my heart, to study in Babylon and Greece and then return to the land. [5]Upon my departure, Baruch gave me this scroll along with the scrolls of my father, and this is how they came to be in my hands.

[6]I vividly remember the day of my mother's death. [7]She lay in the arms of Jeremiah and he whispered many secrets and amorous murmurings into her ears. Watching them, I learned about love. [8]A moment before she passed, she lifted her arm and pointed to the sky, while a smile played upon her lips. [9]I turned my head to see, and I truly expected to see that the sky had parted, and chariots and hosts of angels were coming to escort her to God's

gleaming palace. [10]However, I saw nothing but pale blue and a dusting of white. And when I turned my head back, [11]I saw that she had gone and been gathered to her kin in the way of all the living under the sun.

[12]Every day for years that followed I troubled myself over what she had seen, over what I had missed. [13]One day I asked Baruch, for perhaps he knew something of her visions that I did not. For I had no such visions. [14]Baruch said, "Perhaps she saw nothing. Nothing at all. Perhaps she just wanted you to look away, so that you would not see her die. [15]She saw many people die. She saw her own mother die, Ben Zera. [16]Perhaps she wanted to save you from seeing. Save you from fearing the way she feared." [17]I was satisfied with this, and comforted for the rest of the day, until Baruch tucked a blanket over me late in the night and whispered into my sleepy head, [18]"Or maybe she saw everything. Maybe she saw Eden, and bands of messengers come to bear her up." [19]And so, I lament to this day that I have had no such visions.

[20]To this very day the women of the land come to the tomb of Anatiya my mother to pray. [21]Brides kneel before her grave on the mornings of their weddings and there they shear their hair. [22]I have seen them sprinkle the long locks of their youth over her grave as an offering, that they might have a love at least half as strong.

[23]Though I knew my mother's touch but two years of my life, and my father's touch not at all, I believe they taught me well in the ways of knowledge and wisdom. [24]They imprinted my soul with their art and their ardor for words spoke or writ. I too have written books. [25]In my life I have pursued equanimity between the arduous pursuit of wisdom and the sustenance of a strong family. [26]I cannot give credence to one over the other. [27]Without flour, there is no Torah. Without Torah, there is no flour. These are two ingredients for a good life.

[28]This is where I would end my note, but Anatiya said there are three. [29]She wrote in a letter to me: "This I know. There are three things we must observe to live a good life. Love God. Create family. Pursue wisdom." [30]I know family and I know wisdom, but you put "Love God" at the head. And you wrote it big. [31]But how to love the Instrument that snuffed you out? [32]You must return and teach me, your suckling, how to find that essential piece. [33]I know it is in here somewhere, drowning in your poetry, and one more enlightened and less bound than me perhaps could draw

it out. [34]O, Pharaoh's daughter, wading beside the reeds! The hem of your skirt is muddied. There is a babe in swaddling linens, nestled in a basket of pitch. [35]Did you find him, and did you love him? [36]Or did you slip into the banks and drown and dream it all, one long hallucination of redemption and love. [37]Is it enough to believe in love, daughters, must I believe in God as well? [38]I have been lost in perfumed tresses, locked in soft arms creamy with balm. [39]Grecian eyes have wept for me and Babylonian brides have blushed. [40]But I have not found that love that lives above breathing. Envy of envies. I want it. Immortal elixir. [40]Is it, love, in the trenches of your sea? Is it in Anatot? In you? In prophets? [41]Else I cannot write another word,

answer me